A Crowe Among the Magpies

CHARLIE CROWE

EDITOR
MIKE KIRKUP

Printed and Published by
TUPS BOOKS

Publishers   TUPS
30 Lime Street
Newcastle upon Tyne
NE1 2PQ
Tele: 0191 233 0990
Fax: 0191 233 0579

Distributors   TUPS BOOKS
Newcastle upon Tyne

ISBN **1 901237 05 2**

ACKNOWLEDGEMENTS
The author is grateful to the Dowling family and Billy Pitt for their
help. Thanks also to all the many newspapers who allowed us to
print their articles and photos from the past; and to Jackie
Milburn's sister, Jean Leithead, for her collection of cuttings.

All royalties from this book will be donated to the
Jackie Milburn Memorial Trust Fund, which aims to help
disabled children of the North East.

Registered Charity No 100340
Office - 5 Aqua Terrace, Newbiggin by the Sea, NE64 6PB

CONTENTS

'HERE LIES SIR JOHN'

It was to be my big day: a presentation to the crowd at St James' Park prior to a Division Two game against Swindon Town in October, 1992.

Ruth and I arrived at the ground in good time for lunch in one of the hospitality rooms at the ground. It was full of business executives who had paid a lot of money for the privilege of a buffet lunch, followed by a seat in the directors' box to see the game.

The room could hold about forty people comfortably, but the lure of live television (the game was on Sky TV) had swelled the attendance to a shoulder-to-shoulder sixty folks.

Trevor Garwood, the club's liaison man then, took good care of us and explained what would happen later. After lunch, and about ten minutes before kick off, I was to go on the pitch and be introduced to the crowd. After the match and light refreshments, Trevor was to take us to the main boardroom to receive an inscribed pen from the chairman, Sir John Hall.

I had met Sir John before and found him to be friendly and courteous. But what I noticed about him that day was his restless energy; he seemed to want to talk to everybody in the room at the same time. On occasions he would excuse himself, saying: 'I'll be back in a few minutes.'

Soon it was time to go on the pitch. It was a good crowd of around thirty thousand and the welcome from the Geordie supporters was loud and warm - we always got on well together.

After the game and two false alarms, Trevor got the nod to take us up to the boardroom for the presentation. Sir John welcomed Ruth and I, and, after a chat, he said: 'I would like to give you this inscribed pen, Charlie'. He then introduced us to his wife, Lady Mae, and soon she and Ruth were in earnest conversation. They chatted about the Hall's world tour which had been televised in the *'Around the World'* holiday programme. Sir John turned to me and said:'I've just had a call, Charlie. I will be back in a few minutes.'

'Please forgive him,' said Mae, 'he's always like this.'

A short while later, Ruth reminded me that it was time to go. As we were leaving I said to Lady Mae: 'When Sir John eventually leaves this earth, a fitting epitaph on his headstone should read:

'Here lies Sir John ... he will be back in a few minutes.'

The welcome was loud and warm.

FOREWORD

I first met Charlie Crowe when my father brought Charlie and fellow Newcastle United player, Andy Donaldson, to our house. This was after a card game with the pair in the Conservative Club, just off Sandyford Road, Newcastle. I was 12 years of age, and Charlie was already making his presence felt at St James' Park along with the likes of Jackie Milburn, Frank Brennan, Ernie Taylor, Tommy Walker, Bob Corbett and Bobby Cowell. They, and many more, remained Charlie's lifelong friends.

Having become an ardent supporter of Newcastle United two years earlier, I looked upon Charlie as one of my heroes and he showed me great kindness over the next few years, bringing me autographs and photos which I still retain and treasure to this day. He also told me to come and knock on the players' door whenever I attended an away game; he would come out and give me a ticket for the match. I took him at his word and as a youngster visited grounds all over the country. Charlie never once let me down.

Just over 40 years after we met, I had the privilege of joining the Board of Directors of Newcastle United, and I like to think had the opportunity to repay Charlie for some of his earlier good deeds. Once, while in the company of Sir Stanley Matthews, I asked him about his toughest opponents and he had no hesitation in singling out Charlie, and telling me had never had a good game against him.

This supports the entry in Newcastle United's *Who's Who: Charlie Crowe was a tenacious, hard-working wing half who never gave up the challenge.*

He belongs to the exclusive membership of a Newcastle United side that every Geordie can recite at a moment's notice. He is a founder member of the Jackie Milburn Memorial Trust Fund whose object is the relief of disabled children.

Charlie remains an expert Bridge player and still has a keen eye for any up-and-coming youngsters on the football field. His services are still much in demand as a scout and for his match reports, including his appraisal of future opposition. His reading of a game is second to none, and he remains revered in the North East. Indeed, he is so well known in the area that it would prove difficult to walk the length of Northumberland Street in less than an hour because of the number of people wanting to talk to him about former colleagues or just Newcastle United in general.

I am proud to be a friend of Charlie Crowe and honoured that he asked me to write this Foreword. Because of the distance between us we don't meet often enough these days, but we manage at least twice a year. These meetings will continue to be red-letter days in my diary.

I know that *A Crowe amongst the Magpies* was originally intended for only family and friends, but once the North East discovers its presence it will become as much sought-after as a place on the terraces used to be when Charlie Crowe and his colleagues ran out of the St James' Park tunnel almost half a century ago.

Peter Mallinger (Former Vice Chairman of Newcastle United FC, now Chairman of Kettering Town FC)

INTRODUCTION

I was born in 1924, quite appropriately, I think, within half a mile of St James' Park. The area of Tyneside I grew up in as a lad owed a lot to the Romans: Battlefield and Shieldfield, so it was only natural, I suppose, that I would become involved in some great battles when I played for Newcastle United during their *Glory Days* of the Forties and Fifties.

In 1943 I had played in the same trial match as the legendary Jack Milburn who later became a close friend and colleague. Initially, I had only signed amateur forms. Before then I played schoolboy football with Victoria Jubilee and Newcastle Boys.

When the second world war began I was working as an office boy for Tyne Tees Shipping Company, but later became an apprentice pattern maker at Walker. As a youth I played for Byker and Heaton, and Wallsend St Luke's.

I made my debut for the Magpies in 1945 against Stoke City.. And I was most proud when the *Newcastle Journal* singled me out for praise when we swamped them by nine goals to one; the paper said I was largely instrumental in stifling the talent of the great Stanley Matthews.

As a left-half, not noted for standing on ceremony when it came to a crunching tackle, I recall what our manager in the late 1940s George Martin used to say in his team talk: "Charlie ... the usual," and he then slammed one fist down hard on the palm of his other hand. A man of few words was George.

But it was Stan Seymour who was at the helm when I won my first FA Cup-winners medal in 1951. I missed the 1952 Final after drifting out of favour, was to play in the 1955 Final against Manchester City when I did my ankle in the week before in a game at White Hart Lane against Spurs. Needless to say, I was gutted, but Newcastle came up trumps and ordered that another winner's medal be struck for me.

The highlight of my time at Newcastle came in 1954 when the players got together and chose me to be captain.

Almost at the end of my playing days, I became captain of Third Division Mansfield Town in 1957, going on a free transfer. But I retired from football the next season and came back to the north-east shortly afterwards to become part-time manager of Whitley Bay.

I had a variety of jobs after my footballing days ended including acting as a rep for a building firm and had a spell as a manager with the Scottish and Newcastle Breweries. I ended my working days in 1989 as an Accommodation Officer with the DHSS at Longbenton, only yards away from where I am now living with my wife Ruth who I had married in 1947. We have two daughters: Lesley and Cathy, and twin boys Charles and Simon. Between them they have provided Ruth and myself with ten lovely grandchildren and (at time of writing) two great-grandchildren.

One thing saddens me, however. Of the whole 1951 United team only three men are still alive: Jack Fairbrother, Tommy Walker and I.

Well, that's my story up to date. But I always kept a diary of incidents which happened both on and off the field at St James' Park. I hope you enjoy reading a few of them.

Charlie Crowe. March, 1998

2

I was only three years old when Newcastle United won the First Division title in 1927 with a team that included names like Hughie Gallacher and Stan Seymour. Little did I know then the part that both these footballing giants would play in my later life.

In 1932 when United won the FA Cup, I was only just putting my foot on the first rung of the soccer ladder, playing junior football for the Victoria Jubilee School at Walker.

Towards the end of the 1930s I had left school and found employment for a shipping company as an office boy, still enjoying my football on a Saturday afternoon playing for a couple of youth teams.

Then along came a little German fella with a funny 'tache who threw a spanner in the works,

and football of all kinds began to grind to a halt. Newcastle United, having been ignominiously relegated into the Second Division of the Football League, suddenly found themselves in a regional wartime league which included footballing minnows like Gateshead and Grimsby.

In spite of wartime demands on the team, Newcastle still had a nucleus of great players who had graced St James' Park in the 1930s.

SAM WEAVER

Being a wing-half, it was always my job to take throw-ins, and I was always striving to get some distance into my throw. But from the facts and figures kept by training staff at the ground it was obvious that nobody could ever get near the record throws of Sam Weaver, the Newcastle and England left-half. The test consisted of standing 25 yards from the goal and clearing the crossbar. No mean feat with the heavy leather balls used at the time.

NORMAN SMITH

Norman was Newcastle's trainer for over 30 years. He had coached in Switzerland after finishing his playing career with Sheffield Wednesday in 1937. He joined Newcastle shortly after the war started.

He was the first fully qualified physiotherapist in the football league. But he was apt to get a bit agitated when standing on the touchline during a game, shouting instructions to the players who seemed not to take any notice of him. One day I said to him: 'Norman, the reason we are not taking notice is that the noise of the crowd shuts everything out. We canna hear you, man!'

Grimsby goalkeeper MOULSON is shown saving a shot from Stubbins (stripes) Newcastle United, at St. James's Park, this afternoon.

ONE OF UNITED NINE GOALS

JOY AND SORROW at St. James's Park. The joyful one is Clifton (stripes), on ground as he shoots one of Newcastle United's nine goals. Obviously feeling sorry in the position is Herod, the Stoke goalkeeper.

I was proud to have made my official debut for Newcastle in that 9-1 thrashing of Stoke City. When it came to notching goals, the man on the right in the top photo, Albert Stubbins, was the daddy of them all. Soon after that photo was taken, Albert was signed by Liverpool. He later went on to be the first soccer coach in the USA.

JOE RICHARDSON

Joe was a hard full-back who took no prisoners and was always well groomed when he ran out to play. I played right-half in front of him a couple of times during the war.

But Joe did not like my excursions up the field and told me so. When the war ended Joe retired from playing and was appointed reserve team trainer.

One night I was sparring with him in the gym. The club's unwritten rules of boxing stated that there had to be blows only to the body - no faces. Now Joe had a superb physique and I could not hurt him at all, but he could inflict serious pain on me.

Frustrated with this, I hit him with a right cross, straight in the mouth. He chased me round and round the gym shouting what was going to happen to me once he got his hands on me. But when he calmed down and I explained that my body punches were having no effect, he saw my point. Joe could stand still and let any of the young players punch him in the stomach - he was a tough cookie!

TOM SWINBURNE

Tom was first choice goalkeeper for many years in the 1930s and '40s. He was a warm-hearted character but so unpredictable, at times making brilliant saves only to fumble a simple shot minutes later.

But he used to pride himself on his judgement of free-kicks. Sometimes when the ball was still in flight he would anticipate that it would clear the crossbar, and would go behind to collect the ball from the crowd.

One game against Burnley at Turf Moor was played on a mud heap. A free-kick was awarded to the home team about 30 yards from goal.

The United players all hoped that Tom would not get up to any antics. But as the kick was struck, Tom decided that it was going over the crossbar and he turned around to go behind the goal to retrieve it.

But the ball hit the crossbar and rebounded back into the penalty area where it was scrambled to safety. That was a talking point for many years afterwards. Football people often say that all goalkeepers are mad.

HARRY CLIFTON

Harry was captain of United when I played my first game. He told me of an incident which happened in the 1938/39 season. It seems that the team had a lot of rivalry from within its own ranks, but it was of a religious variety.

Irish centre-half Dominic Kelly was a staunch Catholic while Jock Park, a red-faced, bustling winger, was Protestant through and through. One day, following a heated argument, Dominic finished astride Park with his hands around the Scotsman's throat, saying: 'Say God Bless the Pope and I'll let ye go.'

'God Bless King Billy,' shouted Jock Park, defiantly.

The players had to pull the two apart or things could have got nasty. After that Park stayed away from the ground for three days until the manager had a word with both players and peace was restored.

One day Harry and his wife Kathy called at a country pub for a quiet drink. But they had only been seated a few minutes when a group of Newcastle supporters came in and sat quite close to them.

After a while Harry heard his name mentioned by a rather loud-mouthed individual who said:

'Oh, aye, take it from me, that Harry Clifton drinks far too much. I should know cos I'm one of his best pals. But he doesn't take any notice of me when I tell him.'

Harry got up to order some drinks and as he passed the table where the fans sat, he said to the noisy one: 'What would you like to drink, *pal*?'

This fella, annoyed at being interupted, said: 'No thanks. I don't know you, do I?'

'Of course you do! I'm Harry Clifton and you are one of my best friends.'

You could have heard a pin drop. And then one of the group looking at Harry said: 'Hey, it is, you know. It *is* Harry Clifton! Sorry about that, man, come on let us buy you a drink.'

The know-all supporter's face went red, and obviously embarrassed, he quietly left the room.

In a pre-season practice match in 1945, I was directly opposed to Harry Clifton. He had helped me enormously with my football during the previous season. Before this game he said to me: 'We will see how you cope today, young Crowe.

Well, true to his word, he gave me a hard time and as we left the field at half-time he gave me a knowing wink. I had marked him very tightly, but he never once made an attempt to turn and beat me, playing the ball first time instead, backwards, sideways and using deft flicks. He certainly demonstrated to me the art of playing a ball first time. I came into the game a little better in the second half. Harry had taught me a lesson that I would never forget.

Harry Clifton was signed from Chesterfield in 1938 for £8,500, a club record fee; he played for England against Scotland in 1939 and captained Newcastle on many occasions. He left Newcastle United in 1946 after they had bought Roy Bentley from Bristol City.

He is seen in the photo below leading out the Newcastle team in 1943; behind him is Albert Stubbins, Bob Corbett, Tom Swinburne, Tot Smith, Bob Donaldson, Jimmy Gordon, George Hair, Bob Cowell, Charlie Wayman and on the extreme right is a young Jackie Milburn.

An Agreement

made the _Seventh_ day of _June_ 19 4 7 between **FRANK G. WATT.** of _St. James Park_ in the city. COUNTY OF _Newcastle-on-Tyne._ the Secretary of and acting pursuant to Resolution and Authority for and on behalf of the **NEWCASTLE UNITED.** FOOTBALL CLUB of _Newcastle-on-Tyne._ (hereinafter referred to as the Club) of the one part and _Charles Alfred Crowe_ of _Walker_ in the City County of **Newcastle-on-Tyne.** Professional Football Player (hereinafter referred to as the Player) of the other part **Whereby** it is agreed as follows :—

1. The Player hereby agrees to play in an efficient manner and to the best of his ability for the Club.

2. The Player shall attend the Club's ground or any other place decided upon by the Club for the purposes of or in connection with his training as a Player pursuant to the instructions of the Secretary, Manager, or Trainer of the Club, or of such other person, or persons, as the Club may appoint. [This provision shall not apply if the Player is engaged by the Club at a weekly wage of less than One Pound, or at a wage per match.]

It was a memorable day when I was offered a contract by Newcastle in June, 1947. But, because I was on part-time to begin with, I only received £8 wages during the season and this dropped to £5 a week in the summer months.

TRIAL MATCH, 1943

I was invited for a trial with Newcastle United just before the 1943/44 season got under way. I left home early to get to St James' Park in plenty of time, being unsure of the procedures to follow.

As I approached the players' entrance, a solitary figure was sitting on the steps eating what looked like a pork pie. We introduced ourselves. During the game, I played centre-half on one side while this tall stranger was at inside-left for the opposition In the second half he scored six great goals. And that was why Jack Milburn was snapped up as a professional and walked into the first team at Bradford the following week while I had to be content with signing for Newcastle on amateur terms.

NEWCASTLE 9 - STOKE 1, 1945

What a way to make my debut for the Magpies! Playing against Stoke City with the famous Stanley Matthews in their line-up.

In the event, we won easily with Albert Stubbins our brilliant centre-forward scoring five times. But the whole team played well and at the final whistle our captain, Harry Clifton, walked off the field with his arm around my shoulders.

The *Newcastle Journal* reporter said: '*Crowe was instrumental in blotting out the dangerous Matthews.*'

The attendance that day was 48,000. The rest of the team were professionals and received £3 each, but, as I was still an amateur, I had to claim expenses from the club secretary, Frank Watt.

I received the princely sum of two shillings and sixpence, made up of 1/6 tea money and 1/- travelling expenses. At the time I thought it was a little unfair.

AN EVENTFUL YEAR, 1947

On Boxing Day, 1947, I broke my ankle in a game against West Bromwich Albion. I attended the ground for treatment every day, although my leg was encased in a plaster cast. The club invited me to travel with the team for FA Cup training at Seahouses, even though I was still injured. But after a great Cup run United went out to Charlton Athletic in the semi-final.

Photo on next page shows that it was milk all round for the Newcastle squad up at a farm near Seahouses.

I was married to Ruth in March that year and she gave birth to a baby girl, Lesley, the following January.

George Martin was appointed manager in May, 1947, and a year later took United back into the First Division, but not before making some controversial decisions. Within four months of his arrival he had disposed of Len Shackleton, Tommy Pearson, Charlie Wayman and Roy Bentley, all class performers.

The year of 1947 was also the year that the reserve team won the Central League for the first time in the history of Newcastle United

NEARLY A MAJOR SHAREHOLDER

Our first home was a flat rented to us by a Miss Bell who was an in-law of George Rutherford, chairman of Newcastle United in 1947.

Shortly after Lesley was born, Miss Bell, called to see Ruth who afterwards found some money had been left in the baby's pram which was customary at the time.

The next day I called at Miss Bell's house to thank her for the gift. Imagine my surprise when she asked if I would like to purchase some Newcastle United shares. I asked 'How many and at what price?' I was pleasantly surprised at

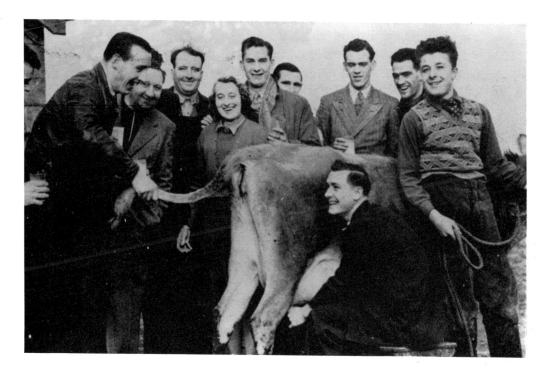

her reply and accepted her offer. She said that she would inform her solicitor. Shortly afterwards I was asked to call and see George Rutherford who said the family solicitor had telephoned him about the proposed sale of shares and asked for further information. I told him that Miss Bell had offered to sell me some of her shares and that I had accepted.

'But, Charlie, don't you know that players can not hold shares?'

'Well, if that's the case,' I replied, 'can I not put them in my wife's name?'

After a long pause he told me that Miss Bell should have known better because the shares belonged to the whole Rutherford family.

If that deal had gone through, I would have held more shares than a few of the then directors. The share capital of the club then was £1,000, made up of 2,000 x 50p shares.

FOOTBALLERS' WAGES, 1947

The maximum wage for top professionals at Newcastle then was £10 a week in the playing season and £8 a week in the summer. Other pros received £10 a game if selected for the first team, but they had to negotiate terms for playing in the reserves and also summer wages.

Jack Fairbrother told me that while he was at Preston North End their reserve goalie Jimmy Gooch was not happy with the terms offered to him and asked Jack for advice. Fairbrother knew that there was nothing between the two of them in terms of ability, so he said: 'Go back and tell them you want the same money as me.'

When Jimmy Gooch spoke to the manager he flatly refused, saying Jack was a better goalie. 'Ah, yes,' said Jimmy, 'but he's not a better goalie than me in the summer!'

Two action shots from the past

That's me in the sandwich at Old Trafford between our goalie Ronnie Simpson and Manchester United's bustling centre-forward, Jack Rowley.

'HOW'S YOUR FINGER, CHARLIE?'

In 1947 I received my National Service papers and immediately informed the club. Stan Seymour arranged with the National Coal Board for me to serve two years as a joiner at Burradon Colliery. It was a ploy used with many Newcastle players, including grammar-school educated Len Shackleton who worked alongside Jackie Milburn at Hazelrigg Workshops.

While at Burradon I suffered a minor cut to my finger which required a couple of stitches. The colliery agent there was Sam Potts.

A couple of days later I was having a bite to eat at the pit canteen when Mr Potts called in, asking: 'Is Charles Crowe here?' He had to ask that question because the canteen was always shrouded under a haze of coal dust,

'Yes, I'm here, Mr Potts,' I replied, suddenly appearing out of the fog.

'Ah, Charles, how is your finger today?'

This was greeted with hoots of laughter from the colliers and surface men.

Two weeks later playing at St James' Park I was taking a throw-in when a supporter yelled: 'How is your finger, Charlie?'

NEWCASTLE FANS

My contact with the fans was always close through taking throw-ins and free-kicks on or near the touchline. If I misplaced a pass or bungled a tackle they would have a go at me: 'Had a beer too many last night, eh?' 'What's wrong, bonnie lad?' 'How's your lass keepin', Charlie?'

But the banter was all tinged with humour. My Dad, a lifelong supporter of the black 'n' whites, used to tell me about the exploits of Newcastle greats like Sam Weaver, Hughie Gallacher, Colin Vietch and Bill McCracken, etc.

I replied: 'Dad, when I finish playing I'll be able to tell the grandbairns about the magic of Stan Matthews, Wilf Mannion, Len Shackleton, Tom Finney, Albert Stubbins, Jackie Milburn, wee Ernie Taylor, Bob Mitchell and big Duncan Edwards, to name but a few.'

CHARLIE WAYMAN

Charlie was the first Newcastle inside-left that I played with. He was a clever ball player and one of the finest dribblers of a ball in the game. Above all, he loved scoring goals, and in his career notched over 250. His strike rate for United was 70 per cent.

Yet still George Stobbart was preferred to Wayman for the semi-final clash with Charlton Athletic in 1947. Tongues began to wag. Charlton won 4-0 and it was an extremely unhappy dressing room afterwards. Doug Wright, our international left-half, flung his boots to the other side of the room, saying: 'Well, that's the nearest I shall ever get to Wembley Stadium.'

A few weeks later Charlie Wayman was transferred to Southampton for £10,000. When asked why he wanted a transfer, he gave this reply: 'Cos I canna find a peg in two dressing rooms to hang my clothes when we are training.' Charlie had to travel from a Durham pit village by bus and always arrived five minutes late for the training sessions. At that time about 35 players used to report for training.

But it was still a bizarre reason for wanting a transfer! Charlie went on to play for Preston and Middlesbrough, winning an FA Cup medal with Preston North End at Wembley.

Left to right, the players are Brennan, Crowe, Pace and Simpson.

HUGHES, the Bolton Wanderers' outside right, had little chance of getting through the defence of BRENNAN, Newcastle centre half, and CROWE, the Tynesiders' left half.

If Ronnie Simpson
failed to get to a high
ball, you can bet that
big Frank Brennan
would be there to save
the day.

BIG FRANK BRENNAN

Frank Brennan arrived at Newcastle United in 1946 with a big reputation and an appetite to match. In his first season on one of our away fixtures, after having an evening meal, the team used to go to the cinema or theatre. But Frank ate all the players' suppers after slipping away and returning to the hotel first. The supper was always laid out in large silver tureens, plates of sandwiches, coffee pots etc.

Frank apologised to everyone, saying: 'All I did was to ask at the reception desk: 'Where do we eat? and they directed me here.'

We all looked at each other, shaking our heads, but there was no answer to that.

Travelling on a summer tour to America on the Queen Mary, he sampled every item on the lunch menu. Touring Ireland in 1948, Frank ate, on average, *ten* eggs every morning with his breakfast.

BIG FRANK AND THE BIG SYRINGE

Before a home match at St James' Park in the late 1940s Frank reported to trainer Norman Smith, saying: 'You'll ha'e to get somebody else to play this afternoon, Norman. Ma back is dead sore and I canna bend down at all.'

Norman was used to Frank's wee tales. He said: 'Not to worry, Frank, I'll get Doctor Bob to have a look at ye.'

After a few minutes Norman returned with Bob Rutherford, the club doctor.

'OK, big fella, strip to the waist and let me have a look at this back of yours.'

After a short examination, the doctor asked Frank to touch his toes. But it was pitiful to watch as Frank went through the motions, barely reaching his knees.

At this point, Doctor Bob said: 'Mmmm ... it looks quite painful, but I think I can give you some ease.' He opened his bag and brought out the biggest syringe that I have ever seen, (it was obviously for use on horses), saying: 'I will just give you a quick jab with this painkiller, Frank, and you'll be as right as rain.'

Frank's eyes had been focused on that massive syringe ever since the Doc had taken it out of his bag. The big Scot began to move sideways and backwards, stretching his back, arms and legs. Drawing himself up to his full height of 6 ft 4 ins, Frank said, meekly: 'Norman, it feels a lot better now, and the pain has gone. Ye knaa what ... I think I *will* be fit to play after all.'

While waiting on the platform at Newcastle's Central Station prior to leaving for London and then flying off to tour South Africa for a ten-week tour in 1952. big Frank was the only one missing.

Norman Smith was prowling around the platform looking for him. Frank arrived just as the train was pulling in. 'Come on, Frank,' moaned Norman, 'you have only just made it.'

As they were boarding the train, Norman realised that Frank had no luggage. 'Where on earth is your gear, Frank, lad?'

'Och, I've go it right here,' said Frank, pointing to the tooth brush protruding from his blazer pocket. He hadn't even brought any toothpaste.

Stan Mortenson, a Geordie lad who made good for Blackpool and England, was discussing big Frank with some of his Lancashire colleagues in the bath after a gruelling match against Newcastle.

'Do you see those bruises, lads? I'm telling you straight - if I had to play agains Frankie Brennan every week I would retire from the game.'

RECORD PRACTICE MATCH, 1946

It seems amazing today but way back in 1946 a pre-season practice game at St James' Park drew a record crowd of 27,763. And it just shows the strength of the squad when some experienced players couldn't even get a game.

STRIPES: Garbutt, Craig, Graham, Harvey, Brennan, Wright, Milburn, Bentley,Stubbins, Wayman and Pearson.

WHITES: Swinburne, Cowell, Corbett, Woodburn, Smith, Crowe, Rushton, McNichol George King, Brown and Nevins.

Other players who attended: Cam Theaker, Ray King, Ron Batty, Don Harnby, John Newton, Bob and Andy Donaldson, George Hair, Ernie Taylor, Tommy Walker, Ron Sales, Les Porter, Tommy Thompson, George Moses, Norman Dodgin and Ernie Whittle. Talk about strength in depth!

STOKE CITY v NEWCASTLE, 1946

After Stoke had beaten us 3-1, Stan Seymour who was then honorary manager told the press: 'Stan Matthews gave the finest display I have ever seen from a winger.'

During the game, Matthews had Bobby Corbett and myself running into each other. Once I didn't think that Stan had the ball under control, so I put in a tackle only to find that the ball and Stan had long gone.

Wilf Mannion of Middlesbrough was the only other player who did that to me. Nobody was safe with Stan in this mood. On one diagonal run he had Jimmy Gordon our right-half tackling and jabbing at the ball to no avail.

A newspaper headline screamed out: *'Matthews showed Corbett and Crowe the maker's name on the ball.'*

DOUG GRAHAM, NEWCASTLE, 1940-50

Doug was nicknamed the 'Baron' and sometimes the 'Duke' on account of his immaculate dress sense - certainly the best dressed man at the club.

I played in front of Doug in the late 1940s, a stylish full-back who read the game well and was a good positional player.

He was also an accomplished sprinter, taking part in many foot handicaps, which many of the Newcastle players did during the close season.

Doug was having his best spell at the club when he had two serious injuries, and was finally transferred to Preston North End in 1950, just as we were embarking on one of our FA Cup runs. After a spell with Lincoln and Gateshead, Doug Graham went into the motor car wholesale trade.

BOB FRASER, NEWCASTLE, 1947-50

Bob was signed from Hibernians to cover for big Frank Brennan in 1947. This he did, but also played a number of games at right full-back.

When George Martin was appointed manager, he wanted to transfer Bob straight away. But Bob told him he was not interested in moving.

After a period of severe pressure from the manager, Fraser asked for a meeting to clear the air, saying to Martin: 'I am going to stay put at Newcastle United, no matter how hard you try to get rid of me. In fact, I'll tell you something else: I shall probably be here long after *you* have gone!'

Bob Fraser was proved right after retiring from playing in 1950 through injury, but then Newcastle made him their chief scout, a position he held for many years after manager Martin had departed.

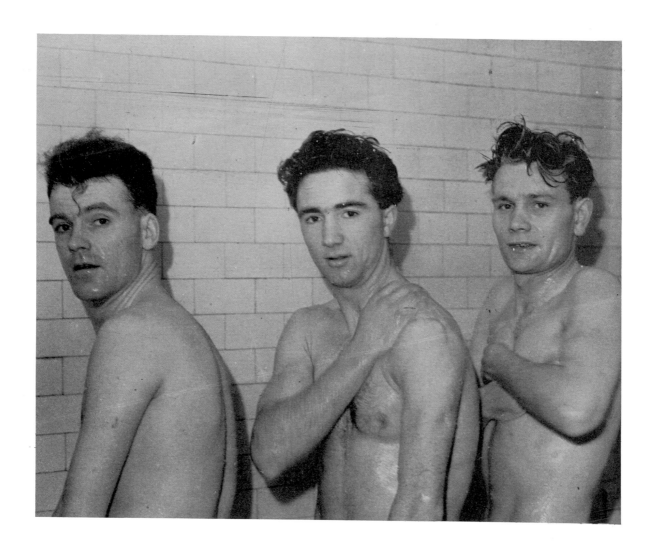

Alf McMichael, Tom Casey and I doing the 'Full Monty'. Newcastle players were so popular that we couldn't even go into the shower without some photographer putting in an appearance.

JOE HARVEY

When Joe Harvey was transferred from Bradford City for £4,200 in 1945 he was introduced to the United players by Stan Seymour.

Joe was dressed in his army uniform. Apart from some old hands like Harry Clifton, Albert Stubbins and Tom Swinburne, the rest of us were aged between 18 and 20. Joe said later that he thought he had joined a youth club team. More of Joe later.

ROY BENTLEY

We were playing Southampton at the Dell in 1947 when Roy, our inside-right, was injured in a clash with one of their defenders. Doctor Bob Rutherford was called from the directors' box to attend to him.

I was reserve for that game and accompanied our trainer Norman Smith to the dressing room. Roy had received a nasty cut above the eye which was bleeding heavily and his eye was rapidly closing.

Doctor Bob came in dressed in his usual navy-blue pinstripe suit and matching waistcoat. He examined Roy and, turning to Norman, said: 'It will need a few stitches, Norman, so clean up the wound and prepare him.'

The Doc was a heavy smoker, and his waistcoat was always stained with ash from his cigarettes. He then began stitching Roy's eye with a ciggie still in his mouth.

Norman Smith began to get alarmed and said: 'Doc, you are still *smoking*.'

The Doc nonchalantly stubbed the cigarette out, saying: 'Oh, so I am. Sorry, Norman. Er ... sorry, Roy.'

JACK FAIRBROTHER

Jack was a complete extrovert: a man of angles and ropes. While training, he would tie ropes round the goalposts, and mark them at various angles to form possible shooting positions at his goal.

Jack Fairbrother had signed for Preston North End in 1938 and found himself understudy to Harry Holdcroft, a famous international in his day.

During his five-year stint at Newcastle between 1947 - 52, Jack liked to have a little wager - usually only a couple of bob - with the forwards such as Roy Bentley, Jack Milburn and Charlie Wayman, betting them that, from a certain distance outside the penalty area, they couldn't beat him. From 25 yards, these prolific goal-scorers could not put one past him.

Asked why he very rarely dived about in the goalmouth, Jack replied: 'There is no need! I *know* when I'm in the correct position. That's why I have the easiest job in football.'

That sums Jack up: the thinker and the perfect positional goalkeeper.

But one thing Jack did have bother with was the Geordie dialect. Most of the lads on the books when he arrived were still working at local collieries. Jack Milburn, for instance, often worked a double shift on a Friday night so that he could get away to matches the following day.

Milburn only drank hot water when he was thirsty - never tea or coffee, Lancastrian Fairbrother came to me one day scratching his head. 'Hey, Charlie, what the hell is Jack Milburn goin' on about? He keeps askin' me to get him a "cup o' het waata".'

TOT SMITH

Tot often deputised for Frank Brennan at centre-half for Newcastle. But each time he did, no matter how well he played, the press always said: 'Brennan was sorely missed'.

We were playing a league match against Luton in the late 1940s and found ourselves three goals up at half-time. Our forwards had really turned it on, in spite of a soggy pitch.

During our interval cup of tea, Tot was cock-a-hoop, shouting: 'Just let the press say that Frank was missed today.'

In the second half it was Luton's turn to apply pressure and they eventually beat us 4-3. Tot was most upset. He just could not believe that second half performance. Needless to say, the headlines the next day screamed: 'Brennan was sorely missed',

---

HOLE IN ONE

On a non-training day, the United players often found themselves on the nearest golf course in the 1940s. Once we played at Wentworth

Frank Brennan, playing in a foursome, had just finished playing a short blind hole. He rang a bell to let the next group know that the green was clear.

The tee box for the next hole was only about five yards away and Frank waited for any balls to appear. Four golf balls came soaring over the hill, three of them landing on the green and one just short. Frank raced over to the green and knocked one of the balls into the hole, then he drove off with his partners on the next hole.

The ball in the hole belonged to Roy Bentley who had to buy drinks all round, thinking that he had holed in one. Later on that evening, the big fella confessed. Mayhem ensued.

RANGERS v NEWCASTLE, 1945

We played at Ibrox Park in aid of the King George VI Benevolent Fund. I found myself up against the Scottish right-wing pairing of Willy Waddell and Tony Gillick.

Rangers won a corner and I picked the man I was marking, looking out towards the corner flag. Suddenly, I felt a terrific pain in my back, and I collapsed.

Afterwards Norman Smith told me that a Rangers' player on the blind side of the referee had kicked me up the backside, right on the bone. I never forgot that lesson and made a point to be extra careful in future.

Many years after I had stopped playing, Stan Seymour was telling me that Rangers fancied me and had tried to sign me on several occasions. It would have been nice to be told at the time and not twenty years later!

NEWCASTLE 6 GRIMSBY 2, 1945

At half-time we were trailing 1-2. Stan Seymour decided to switch me from the half-back line up to inside-left.

During the second half I scored once and was enjoying my new role. That was until I collided with the 6ft 3ins Betmead, Grimsby's bulky centre-half, and suffered concussion.

Harry Clifton chastised me saying I should pay more attention to what was happening *off* the ball. 'Could you not see, Charlie,' he said, 'Betmead had set himself for you, and you fell straight into his trap.' Another lesson learnt.

'LOOK AT THEM HANDS, CHARLIE'

We were playing at Maine Road, Manchester, in 1947 against City who had that gentle giant of a man, Frank Swift, as their last line of defence.

In one of City's attacks, our goalie, Tom Swinburne, pulled off a truly remarkable save, pushing a pile-driver around the post for a corner.

I had been chasing back to the goalmouth and helped Tom to his feet, saying: 'Well done, Tom. Great save!'

Swinburne, eyes gleaming, replied in all seriousness: 'Aye, Swifty would never have got nowt near that one. Look at them hands, Charlie. Look at them hands. Safest pair of hands in the business.' And all the while he was nodding away to himself, as if to verify what he was saying.

BOBBY COWELL, 1947

Bobby hadn't been all that long in the first team when we played away at Turf Moor against Burnley.

The home side were awarded a free-kick just outside the penalty box. Goalie Swinburne arranged our wall to his liking.

But the free kick took a cruel deflection off Bobby's thigh and flew into the net, leaving Swinburne stranded at the opposite side. The goalie shouted at captain Joe Harvey: 'Get him off the bloody park! Go on, send him packing.'

He then vented his anger on the young full-back: 'Whey, man, the likes of you would never have been allowed outside the dressing room before the war. Go on - get off the field. Get off!' he screamed, pointing towards the touchline.

Joe Harvey intervened and put his arm around Tom Swinburne's shoulder in an effort to pacify the excitable custodian of the nets. 'Never mind, Tom,' said Harvey, 'he's only young, he'll learn.'

But Swinburne went back into goal muttering to himself: 'Bloody full-backs!'

MAN. CITY v NEWCASTLE, 1947

I received the ball on the half-way line, made progress down the left side, and passed the ball to Tommy Walker out on the right touch line.

After I passed, I kept on running and shouted for the return pass. It came back to me, inch perfect. All I had intended to do was to make for the corner and then cross the ball. But when I looked up, City's England international goalie, Frank Swift, was well off his line.

I tried to chip Swift, but, incredibly, he flung himself backwards and sideways. catching the ball in one huge hand; and with the next movement he was on his feet and throwing the ball forty yards to the City forward *I* was supposed to be marking. Amazing!

'I'VE GOT YOU, TAYLOR'

It was during a game at Ayrsome Park in 1948 that I came up against a former colleague, Jimmy Gordon, scourge of all attackers. He had been transferred from United in 1945 after Joe Harvey had been drafted into the team. He later became coach with Brian Clough at Hartlepool. following the controversial Cloughie to Leeds, Derby County and Notts Forest.

Jimmy always let the opposition know that he was around. During this game, Ernie Taylor had dribbled his way through the entire Boro defence and was squaring up to shoot at goal when Jimmy Gordon, all of five yards behind the wee fella, growled: 'I've got you, Taylor. I've got you!'

Ernie got such a shock that he rushed his shot, sending it soaring yards over the bar, much to Jimmy's delight.

IRISH TOUR, 1947

We had gone across to Ireland as part of a close season tour to play a few friendly matches.

One day our party visited Blarney Castle, famous for the stone kissed by strangers - it was supposed to give whoever kissed it, the Gift of the Gab.

Unfortunately, to kiss the stone you had to be held by your legs and suspended upside down through a metal grill. This procedure was carried out forty yards above ground level, so it was certain death if you fell. In fact, so we were informed, several people in the past had done just that by not taking the right precautions.

My big mistake was in saying: 'Oh, I wouldn't mind trying that.'

The players who came forward to hold my legs were the two notorious pranksters of the squad: George Stobbart and Frank Brennan. I sighed with relief when my feet touched *terra firma*.

George Stobbart and I shared a room during the tour. Late one night while in a hotel in Bangor he told me that he had heard my name mentioned.

It seems that he had been in the hotel lounge when manager George Martin and trainer Norman Smith had entered. They failed to spot Stobbart and began to talk heatedly about me. It transpired that Martin wanted to 'put me out of the game if I didn't sign my contract'.

Norman was taking my side. The wages then were still £10 a week in season and £8 in summer. I had only been offered a summer wage of £7-10s so I had refused to sign. When the season got under way and I became a regular in the first team I got my rise and two years later when Martin left to manage Aston Villa he tried to take me with him Villa Park.

LEN SHACKLETON

I recall one day that as I was about to take a throw-in, Len pointed at his backside so that he could knock it back to me. He always wanted to do the difficult things.

One particular game at St James' Park against Cardiff was typical of the way the supporters were treated to the *Shack Magic*.

After a spell of interpassing with Tommy Pearson which demoralised the Cardiff defence, Len actually hitched up his shorts, sat on the ball and brought the game to a temporary halt. The crowd were ecstatic. In the same match he tried to do a one-two off the corner flag!

Shack found himself in favour with England coach Walter Winterbottom in the late 1940s, winning a smattering of England caps. But Len did not suffer fools gladly.

One day, grouped with the rest of the England squad during a training session, Shack had to listen to a team talk by Winterbottom which went something like: 'Now with this move I want you Billy (Wright) to transfer the ball to Tom (Finney) who will send the ball to Wilf (Mannion) then to Jimmy (Mullen). It is then that Jack (Milburn) will go on a dummy run and the ball will be switched back to Tom (Finney) who will get to the bye-line and cross to Len (Shackleton) who will put it into the net.'

There was a long pause before Len piped up: 'Ah, yes, Walter ... but which *side* of the net?'

The Baseball Ground at Derby was notorious for being nearly all sand. Taking a free-kick, Len teed the ball up on a mound of sand. 'You can't do that,' said the ref, 'it doesn't say you can do that in the rules.'

'Ah, yes,' said Len, but there's nothing in the rules to say you *can't* do it either.'

MAGPIES BACK IN DIVISON ONE, 1948

Newcastle United eventually got back into the top flight in 1948 - it was where they belonged. But we made it the hard way. This is how that glorious day was described by Mike Kirkup in his book *Jackie Milburn in Black and White*:

The Magpies had made a great start to the 1947/48 season by beating Plymouth 6-1 with Milburn keeping up a remarkable record of scoring in the first and last league matches for four consecutive seasons.

Eastertime was always crucial and United came out of it in second place behind Birmingham closely followed by Sheffield Wednesday.

By mid April Newcastle were almost there. They had beaten Fulham 1-0 thanks to a penalty by George Stobbart to register their tenth successive home win, and were ready to take on the Sheffield side in the next match. A vast crowd of 66,843 filled the Gallowgate and Leazes terraces almost to bursting point.

With only ten minutes remaining of the crucial game, the teams were level at 2-2 thanks to goals by Stobbart and skipper Joe Harvey. One point was no good to Newcastle - it was win or bust.

Frank Houghton proved an unlikely hero. A half-back turned winger, Houghton scored two goals, breaking his arm in the process of knocking in the second after colliding with a goalpost.

It was all stirring stuff, and the final whistle blew with young Frank still being borne by a stretcher around the pitch perimeter.

But Newcastle United were virtually there. Tyneside went wild when Newcastle officially clinched promotion, albeit in second place behind Birmingham.

1949 team top left: George Martin, Frank Houghton, Joe Harvey, Charlie Crowe, Jack Fairbrother, Frank Brennan, Alf McMichael, Norman Smith. Front: Tom Walker, Bob Cowell, Ernie Taylor, Jackie Milburn, George Robledo and Bobby Mitchell.

To celebrate getting back into the top flight, I bought myself a car:
a second-hand Ford Prefect.

'DOES THE WIFE KNOW?'

In the late 1940s, Newcastle and Bolton had agreed a transfer fee for Bob Langton, the Lancashire club's England international winger.

Before signing, Bob said his wife would like to come and have a look at the North East. But the deal fell through once she had had a close look at Geordieland. Langton told the Newcastle board that it was all off. The *Newcastle Journal* headline the next day read:

Mrs Langton says 'No' to Newcastle

The teams met at St James' Park a few weeks later in a league match. Bob Langton had hardly set foot on the pitch when the crowd began to taunt him: 'Does the wife know where you are?' and 'Mind you hurry home after the game.' Langton took the good-natured banter in his stride.

'MAKE YOUR CROSSES HIGH'

When it came to 'tactics' the United players always took new ideas with a pinch of salt.

One manager said to our immaculate winger Tom Pearson: 'Tom, get to the bye line and make your crosses high to the far post.'

'Why should I do that, Boss?' queried Tom.

'So that the forwards can head for goal. I would have thought that was obvious.'

'Hold on,' replied Tom, 'take a look at our forward line: Milburn, Shackleton, Wayman and wee Ernie Taylor. Now there's not one of 'em exactly noted for heading the ball, is there?'

'Mmmm ... .'

'So why don't I do what I've been doing for the past donkey's years: get to the line and pull the ball back along the ground?'

'Yeah ... you've got a point there, er, Tom. A good point.'

'SHOW 'EM YOUR ARSES'

There was never much done at Newcastle in the Forties with regard to coaching. A typical team talk by manager George Martin before a game went something like:

To Jack Fairbrother: 'Jack ... the 18-yard area ... make it your own ... you're the Boss.'

To Cowell and Corbett: 'Now ... the two Bobs ... these two wingers ... put a rope round their necks.'

To Joe Harvey: 'Joe ... keep 'em going.'

To Frank Brennan: 'Frank ... put 'em in your pocket.'

To Yours Truly: 'Charlie ... give them the usual.' (*Bashing one fist against the other*).

To Walker and Milburn: 'Tom ... Jackie ... show 'em your arses.'

To Ernie Taylor: (*Ruffling Ernie's hair*) 'Ah ... the little man.' (*Nodding his head as if to emphasise some point*).

To George Robledo: 'George ... the far post.'

To Bobby Mitchell: 'Mitch ... the extra man ... don't overdo it.'

'Right then lads ... out you go.'

DEFENSIVE WEAKNESS

We were due to play Blackpool in a league match when George Martin decided that he had discovered a weakness in the Seasiders' defence: left-back Tommy Garrett, a Geordie lad from Horden in county Durham.

'Now lads, the first opportunity you get, I want you to hit as many balls as you can to the right side of the park so that Tommy (Walker) can really go to town on this full-back.'

After the game the local press proclaimed: *Garrett - man of the match.* A month later he was capped for England. Nice one, George!

Newcastle *Journal* comments on Charlie Crowe, 1940s
by Ken McKenzie

v Stoke (won 9-1)

Another factor in the non-success of the Blackpool forwards was the strong play of Newcastle's wing-half Crowe, a Byker youth - a sound worker with the conception of what his forward wanted in support. A stranger within the gates might once or twice have been deceived into thinking that *he* was United's captain.

v Bury (won 4-2)

Cowell tried a shot which Bradshaw saved, and Crowe and Wayman as usual were putting in some hard work. Crowe stopped a menacing Bury move and from his clearance the home forwards started an attack by Milburn and Hair who crossed nicely for Stubbins to head over. Bury's goalkeeper Bradshaw, when troubled by a high shot from Crowe, fisted over the bar.

v Grimsby (won 6-2)

The turning point in the game came when Crowe, the left-half, scored an amazing goal from the line on the right side of the field after having changed places with Gordon. Crowe brought further inspiration into the attack and with Milburn and Hair in sparkling form on the wings the Grimsby defence had a gruelling time.

v Manchester City (drew 1-1)

The 54,000 spectators at St James' Park yesterday were lucky if they saw any of the first half because of the thick fog; for a period of ten minutes the fans were quite in the dark. Of the wing-halves, Crowe had a very good game, both in defence and attack.

v Bradford (won 4-0)

For his terrier-like tactics and the way in which he looked after Shackleton, Bradford's potential match-winner, Crowe ranked as the best half-back on the field. Two goals apiece were scored by Clifton and Stubbins.

v Liverpool (won 6-2)

Newcastle, strengthened by the return of Stubbins, Wayman and Crowe, were meeting old first division opponents whose last visit was in the 1933/34 season. Liverpool were without their left winger Billy Liddell who was playing for Scotland against Wales. From a cross by Milburn, Stubbins failed to connect properly. Crowe cleverly intercepted but his pass to Clifton was handled by Bob Paisley.

'BEHIND YOU, CHARLIE'

We were playing away at St Andrew's against Birmingham who had the reputation of being a very physical side.

As the game progressed, I had been involved in a running battle with Stewart, their Scottish right-winger. In one incident in our penalty area, Jack Fairbrother shouted: 'Behind you, Charlie.'

I turned to see Stewart jumping at me with both feet aimed at my private parts. I took evasive action and was about to retaliate when I was suddenly sent crashing to the ground, not by a Brummie, but by my own colleague, Jack Fairbrother, who was astride of me, pinning my arms.

The referee whose vision had been obscured, rushed to the scene bleeping on his whistle, shouting to me: 'I didn't see everything that happened, Crowe, but one more doubtful tackle from you and you're off.'

Stewart who had got away Scot free heard the ref's remarks and taunted me for the rest of the game. I had to hold myself in check or risk being sent off.

The Birmingham Supporters' Club were so impressed by Fairbrother's actions, which so obviously kept *their* man on the pitch, that they sent a letter to the Newcastle board praising Jack's sportsmanship.

'IT KEEPS HIM IN TOUCH'

In 1949 we played Manchester United at Old Trafford. I was waiting for the ball to be returned so that I could take a throw-in.

As the ball came back it ran towards their centre-forward, Jack Rowley, nicknamed the 'Gunner'. He blasted the ball at me like a bullet. I had been marking Jimmy Morris so I asked him 'Why?'

'Oh,' he replied, 'Jack always does that when he hasn't had a shot at goal for a while - it keeps him in touch.'

GEORGE HANNAH'S TOE POKES

George Hannah made his debut in 1949 playing inside-left in front of me at St James' Park.

The visiting goalkeeper took a goal-kick and the opposing forward and I went for a high ball.

As I jumped, looking around, all I could see was Mitchell on the touchline, closely marked. I had no alternative but to head the ball wingwards and out of play.

When I landed I looked for George, and there he was, standing only a couple of metres. away from me. I fumed at him: 'What do you think you are doing?'

'I'm trying to help you, Charlie,' he said.

'How the hell can I find you with the ball when you're here?'

Although only nine stones in weight, George was a clever schemer with delicate ball skills and a good work rate. One feature of his game was a pass we called the 'Hannah toe-poke'. He would hit the ball with a short jab, and he practised the pass in training and five-a-side games.

When I asked him why, he said: 'Because if I'm slow on the ball I am getting kicked on the ankles far too often.'

George only used the pass in close tight situations on the pitch, and it worked.

Hannah only got into the first team on a regular basis when George Robledo left for Chile in 1953. He won a cup-winners medal with United in 1955, and went on to play 167 games for the Magpies, scoring 41 goals.

It wasn't just the knights on white chargers who fought battles at Gallowgate. This one featured George Hannah and Ron Batty versus Yours Truly aboard the good steed, Tommy Walker.

Hillsborough action in 1950 as Fairbrother punches clear from a Sheffield Wednesday attacker and his team-mate, Frank Brennan. I can only stand and admire the view.

There were not many team talks before a match. But the players below obviously put on a show for the camera in 1948 in the hotel lounge the night before a game at Leicester.
Back left: Charlie Wayman, Tom Swinburne, Roy Bentley, Tom Pearson, Doug Wright, Charlie Crowe, Burke and Joe Harvey.
Front: Norman Smith, George Stobbart, Len Shackleton, Doug Graham, Tot Smith, and Frank Brennan.

'WE FELT SORRY FOR YOU'

We were at home to Huddersfield during the 1948/49 season and torrential rain fell throughout the game. The crowd on the open terraces were drenched.

After the game I had arranged to meet my father at his club in the east end of the city. At that time there were very few private cars around and certainly on that night the majority of the fans used public transport.

As I entered the club I was greeted by a couple of members who had obviously been to the match. One of them called over and said: 'Hey, Charlie, we didn't half feel sorry for you, playing in all that rain.'

OBSCENE LANGUAGE

The return match that season with Huddersfield also proved quite eventful.

A long clearance from the home side went down our right flank. Bobby Cowell and Joe Harvey both went for the same ball, getting themselves in a rare old mix up and both leaving the ball for each other. Metcalfe, the home side's outside-left, nipped in and created havoc in our defence before the ball was eventually cleared.

And while all this was going on, Bob and Joe were going at it hammer and tongs with the air ripe enough to cut with a corneycrake.

Things were so bad that a Huddersfield fan reported them both to the Football Association for using obscene language.

BOB CORBETT

Bob began his career as a winger with Throckley before joining United. He was very quick, running three yards inside even time as a pro sprinter during the summer months.

I played with Bob for about six seasons and we never had an argument - *never*. He played football with a permanent smile on his face, never deliberately committing a foul or troubling the referee.

But in one game against Bolton Wanderers the season after winning the FA Cup in 1951, he uncharacteristically misplaced a pass. Joe Harvey was furious and shouted out in his sergeant-major-style voice: 'Corbett, you're a stupid bastard!'

Bob immediately squared up to Harvey, but after a few seconds tempers cooled and they both laughed and shook hands.

Swearing was like 'God Bless You' to Joe Harvey, and he could not apologise enough afterwards to Bob. But the management saw the incident in a different light and Bob Corbett was transferred to Middlesbrough one month later.

ARTHUR DREWRY, FA

Arthur was FA president and chairman of selectors for the Football Association.

Speaking in 1950 when transfer fees were starting to spiral, he said: 'I consider the present situation to be an unreal period in the transfer market.

'I cannot think that the payment of fees exceeding £30,000, like that paid for Jackie Sewell, will continue. There are some people who advocate that a player should receive a percentage of the transfer fee when he goes from one club to another, but the dangers of such provision are obvious.'

Shortly afterwards there was speculation that Jackie Milburn might leave Newcastle, Stan Seymour said: 'I just start valuing Jackie at £40.000.'

I just *start* valuing 'Wor Jackie' at £40,000!

HOWWAY Jackie! Howway Jackie! That is the victory cry at St. James's Park today. Never has United known such a popular player. How did United secure this "star" of soccer?

It all began with an announcement in the Press that United welcomed young players to attend at St. James's Park for a trial. From Ashington came the youngster Milburn.

I met him for the first time in my life in the club billiard room. He was standing with a little brown paper parcel under his arm. In it were a pair of football boots.

I asked him his name, where he came from, what position he played in, and for whom he had been playing. Later that day I watched him in action in a practice match. Within minutes I knew he had what it takes to make the grade.

I saw him after the match. He had been told to collect his expenses. I was present when Mr. Frank Watt paid him his few shillings.

He was invited to come again. He did, and I was present to see him. I decided then and there he was a future "star."

I told Frank that the youngster Milburn must be put on United's professional strength at once.

A few days later I informed United's secretary I was going

"WOR JACKIE"

to Ashington. Frank asked, "What are you going to do" I replied, "I'm going to sign Milburn."

In a little colliery row I found the Milburn home.

I was welcomed, invited to sit down, and have "a bite of something to eat." Rations were scarce in those days, but the family insisted.

I remember sitting in front of a roaring fire longing to escape, but not without my man. I suffered the agonies of an inferno that day.

Jackie sat near saying little or nothing. His Dad did the talking. Then I boldly asked, "Do you want to become a player for Newcastle, Jackie?"

Before he had time to answer I produced the forms, and in a flash the eager youngster had appended his signature.

He was to be a part timer, for he was working at the pit. It was war-time football. His wage 30s. a match.

We celebrated my capture that night in the working men's clubs of Ashington. I returned, and, full of having done a great job, threw down the forms in front of Mr. Frank Watt and remarked, "I've signed Jackie Milburn, Frank, and I've signed a future England international."

That was, I think, my greatest discovery. Today he is the top price player in the game. My value? Well, begin at £40,000.

For the record, the date of the signing was November 13, 1940. Who said 13 was an unlucky number? Why, that's the number of Jackie's house at Ashington.

Stan Seymour eulogises about 'his greatest discovery', the miner's son from Ashington. But even Stan's memory let him down in the last para: Jack Milburn signed for Newcastle in *1943* (not 1940).

'YOU'RE TOO LATE, JACK'

We were playing a local derby game at Roker Park in 1949 and during a pre-match kick-about the ball came from the Sunderland end towards me. And who should toddle up to retrieve it but the Clown Prince himself, Len Shackleton.

Len hadn't been at Sunderland long after leaving us, and he was still quite pally with most of the Magpie lads.

I handed Len the ball and he said: 'I'll tell you what, Charlie, when you get the ball I shall leave you alone and you can do the same for me.'

'Sorry, Len,' I said, 'but I have had strict instructions to mark you very closely.'

Len shrugged his shoulders and turned away, muttering to himself: 'Bloody Harvey!'

Towards the end of the game, Shack smashed a 30-yard shot past a diving Fairbrother. 'You're too late, Jack,' shouted Len, 'it's in the back of the net!'

Playing against Sunderland and marking Shack was never easy. Apart from his footballing skills he had a barbed sense of humour.

Arthur Hudgell, the Sunderland left-back was having a nightmare, passing the ball to us more than his colleagues. After yet another misplaced pass, Shack shouted across the field: 'No, Arthur,' pointing at his jersey, 'we are the *red* and whites.'

Word began to seep out of Roker about the rivalry and ill-feeling that existed between Shackleton and their Welsh international centre-forward, Trevor Ford. It was said that Len was deliberately giving Ford bad passes and sometimes making him run into offside postions.

The burly striker was alleged to have given boss Bill Murray an ultimatum: 'It's Shack or me, make your mind up.' Back came Murray's reply: 'When are you leaving, Trevor?'

FRED HALL, SUNDERLAND

Sunderland in the late Forties had a hard man stopper at centre-half called Fred Hall, a genial giant who loved his pigeons, and had a beautiful turn of wit.

During one derby game against Newcastle, the ball was switched to Bobby Mitchell on the left wing. The Sunderland right-back then was a guy called Jackie Stelling, a no-nonsense type of player who tackled like a demon.

When Mitch was approaching the Roker-end goal, big Fred shouted: 'He is all yours, Jack.' And away went Stelling, off on a wild goose chase in search of the mercurial Mitchell.

'THAT'S YOUR JOB, CHARLIE'

Bobby Mitchell used to make my job all that much easier, always making himself available, always in space for the easy pass.

But this magnificent ball player, when not actively involved himself, appeared almost disinterested in the game. One day the ball ran out of play just where he was standing. I shouted at him to take a quick throw-in so that we could take an advantage. He turned his back on me and walked away, saying: 'Oh, no, Charlie, that's *your* job, pal.'

Even if the United defence was being hard pressed in a tight game, there would be Mitch nonchalantly putting divots back into place where the ground had been churned up, delicately tapping the turf on the touchline where he used to bewilder the opposition.

Many years later Mitch was tried as a half-back and he was the star player for the rest of the season. After one home game I met him and he greeted me with: 'Hey, Crowe, I thought you said playing left-half was hard - it's a piece of cake!'

30,000 CROWD TO BREAK EVEN

Frank Watt was Newcastle United's secretary for 20 years. I was talking to him before one of our home games and he explained to me how he used to assess the number of spectators in the ground.

'Well, Charlie, when I can see their chests clearly then about 30,000 are present; when I can see their chins then that means 50,000; but if I can only see the whites of their eyes then I know we have 60,000 plus inside St James' Park.'

Frank reckoned that it took a crowd of 30,000 for the club to break even, financially. The visiting team at that time received 50 per cent of the gate receipts which made it a big-money day for the minnows who came to Newcastle.

'HAND ME MY SOCKS, CHARLIE'

During our 1948 close season tour of Ireland we played four matches in two weeks. When on tour we received a special money allowance to cover out of pocket expenses.

In a Dublin hotel after breakfast, we approached Stan Seymour and George Martin to ask if there was any cash. Stan said: 'Oh, you'll have to see Frank Watt - he has all the ready cash with him in his bedroom.'

I knocked on the bedroom door and after a pause Frank shouted for me to come in. I entered the room and he was still lying in bed. 'Stan Seymour said to come up and you would give me some cash to share with the players, Frank.'

'Oh, right-o then, Charlie,' said a voice coming out of the semi-darkness. 'Can you just hand me my socks over, please.'

'Your socks?'

'Aye,' says Frank, 'that's where I keep all the spare cash.'

'NO MORE GORY DETAILS'

We were travelling by coach from Manchester where we had been staying overnight prior to a game at Turf Moor against Burnley in a first division tussle.

I was always a bad traveller and sat in the front seat next to the door so that if I wanted some fresh air I wouldn't disturb anyone. Docotor Bob Rutherford came and sat next to me, asking if there was anything he could do.

After reassuring him that I was OK, he began to relate to me some of his exploits in the first world war when he was a young medical officer in the trenches of France.

And pretty horrific some of his tales were, particularly the one of where he had to cut off the leg of a badly-wounded soldier, using only a clasp knife after sterilising it in a billy can filled with hot water.

On reaching the ground, Norman Smith, noticing my pale face, asked: 'Are you OK, Charlie?'

I told him what had happened and he reported it to the rest of the directors. Shortly afterwards Doctor Bob was sent a memo: 'Please, no more gory details of operations to players before a match.'

'HE'LL BE FIT AS A FIDDLE'

Jimmy Woodburn and I were in for treatment at St James' one morning. In walked Doctor Bob. We were both stripped to the waist and Bob noticed a spot on Jimmy's chest. 'That looks really nasty - just let me take a look at it.'

In spite of Jimmy's protestations, the doc took a knife out of his bag and made a couple of swift incisions. Jimmy yelped with pain.

"That should do it,' said the doc to Norman Smith. 'He'll be fit as a fiddle in no time.'

ERIC GARBUTT

If Eric had not been injured in 1948 with a broken hand and in 1950 with a broken leg which finished his career, he could possibly have been the pick of Newcastle's three keepers at the time.

He had a mixture of Ronnie Simpson's flair and Jack Fairbother's goal-line reflexes. Eric was always in charge coming out for high balls and crosses. He commanded respect, and was a likeable, quiet person.

JOE MERCER

I played against Joe when he was at Everton in 1945, but was introduced to him formally by his old army pal, Joe Harvey, in 1947.

Whenever I was in Joe Mercer's company, I enjoyed his sense of humour and immense knowledge of football.

Joe captained England, Everton and Arsenal before a serious knee injury halted his career. He later went on to be a successful manager with clubs like Sheffield United and Manchester City before being appointed as caretaker manager of the England squad, being able to boast that they never lost a game while he was in charge.

JACKIE ROBINSON

Jackie was born in Shiremoor, a mining village not far from Cramlington.

He signed for Sheffield Wednesday when he was a teenager and was capped for England in 1937 against Finland, making him the youngest player at that time to represent his country.

I played against Johnna, as he was known, when he was with Sunderland, and what a handful he was! Len Shackleton swore that Johnna was the fastest man in the game.

WANTED ANOTHER GO

After another gruelling battle with old rivals at Roker Park, I was first off the field. I was in the bath when Ron Batty came in with his arm around Bob Stokoe's shoulder. I noticed that Bob was bleeding from the mouth.

'What happened to you, Bob?' I asked.

'Oh, I had a few words with Billy Elliott as we were leaving the park and he put the nut in.'

It seems there were conflicting versions of what had actually happened. It was alleged that Stokoe had put two fingers up to the Sunderland man.

Anyway, Stan Seymour took some details and then reported Elliott to the referee who, in turn, reported the matter to the FA.

Stokoe and Elliott had to attend an FA tribunal with Ron Batty as witness. The outcome was that Elliott was found guilty and fined.

After they left the hearing, Elliott wanted another go at Bob Stokoe.

STAN BELL

Stan was a *Newcastle Journal* reporter who covered all the Sunderland games in the late 1940s. But he was intensely disliked by everyone who wore a red and white shirt.

So much so, that, after one match, he went into the dressing room, began to make his mouth go, and was promptly thrown head first into the communal bath. The following week he was moved by his newspaper to cover *our* games.

However, he failed to endear himself to the United players either. But he did curry favours from Stan Seymour who he used to call:

Mr Newcastle.

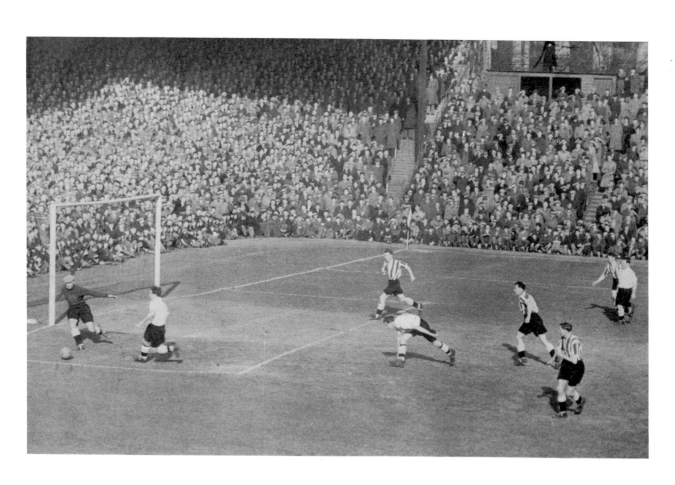

Leazes End incident in 1949 against Derby County. From left: Fairbrother, McLaren (D), Crowe, Stamp (D), Cowell, Walker, Corbett and Morris (D).

RUBBER BOOTS

It was 1949 and we had been playing at Stamford Bridge in one of the early rounds of the FA Cup. The ground was like a skating rink with sheets of pure ice scattered all around.

Roy Bentley, Chelsea's England international who had left United to join the London team, wore a new style lightweight rubber boot, and he skated rings around us.

After the game, Roy gave me the name of the manufacturer and I wore the same boots on icy pitches until I retired.

The photo on left shows Roy Bentley, Billy Wright and Jackie Milburn trying on their rubber boots prior to flying off to Rio to take part in the 1950 World Cup.

It might have been first class to South America, but for the United squad, featured below, it was on the bus to Seahouses!

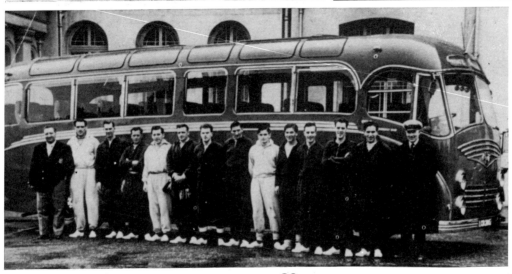

TOP Milburn and Mortenson wonder if their plane will get them to the 1950 World Cup in Rio

BTM Jack and Shack played together for Newcastle and England

37

THE DAILY MAIL; FRIDAY, MARCH 9, 1951

An unusual sight in the market town of Buxton, Derbyshire, yesterday, when members of the Newcastle United team (left to right) Milburn, Harvey, G. Robledo, and Taylor, after leaving their temporary headquarters at a Buxton hotel, trotted through the streets as part of their training in preparation for Saturday's F.A. Cup semi-final against Wolverhampton at Sheffield.

When we were on a successful FA Cup run in the 1950s we often stayed at the Derbyshire spa town of Buxton. We were caught here on a run around the town, but the photgrapher got the names wrong. That's *me* on the right - not Ernie Taylor.

Man in the middle of this Turkish bath party at Newcastle is Donald Peers, and on either side are George Robledo and Jackie Milburn, toning up for Saturday's FA Cup-tie against Bristol Rovers.

FRONT LINE WITH GOALS ALL WAY

By ALAN DALE

WEATHER-WATCHING preoccupies Newcastle United's FA Cup players again. A moderate snowfall at breakfast-time changing to sleet and rain threatens unpleasant conditions for Saturday's tie with the Third Divisionists, Bristol Rovers, and today's golf at Morpeth, which is of more immediate concern to players who have developed a Scottish enthusiasm for the game.

Newcastle United would prefer a lightish field but soft enough to provide a foothold and make ball-control possible.

But they have prospered on mud patches and knocked out Bury on a field partly under water with a foundation of ice.

George Robledo recalled last night noticing some surreptitious movement while the two teams were lined up for that minute's silence at Stoke.

It was the effort of a Stoke player to extricate his feet which had sunk in mud to the eyelet holes in his boots.

George himself scored two of the four goals against Stoke City, Mitchell and Milburn getting the others.

Donald Peers and his *Babbling Brook'* was almost as popular as Newcastle United in the 1950s.

The semi-final against Wolves at Hillsborough was goalless.

'WEMBLEY HERE WE COME'

In a local newspaper article shortly before Newcastle's FA Cup semi-final game with Wolves in 1951, Joe Harvey had predicted that it was to be Newcastle's year for winning the cup.

But the game ended in a goalless draw, as did the other semi between Blackpool and Birmingham.

Our replay was to be held at Huddersfield's ground on March 15th. Teams were:

WOLVES: Williams, Short, Pritchard, Russell, Shorthouse, Wright, Hancocks, Walker, Swinbourne, Dunn and Mullen.
NEWCASTLE: Fairbrother, Cowell, Corbett, Harvey, Brennan, Crowe, Walker, Taylor, Milburn, Robledo and Mitchell.

For a long time that day it was doubtful whether the match would get under way. Incessant rain had flooded the pitch and terraces, and huge pipes were brought in to pump out the water. Minutes before the kick-off the referee declared the pitch fit, but there was no time to clear away the metal pipes, so they were stacked behind the goals.

Wolves shocked us by scoring an early goal through inside-right, Walker. They kept us under severe pressure and Bob Cowell gave away a corner on the right which was quickly taken by their Engalnd winger, Johnny Hancocks.

Big Frank Brennan rose above the Wolves' attack to head clear, but in doing so stumbled and fell off the pitch, banging his head against a metal pipe. Stan Seymour swore he heard the crack up in the directors' box.

Norman Smith raced on to the pitch to where Harvey was bending over the motionless Brennan, whose face had by now turned ashen grey.

Joe turned to Norman and said: 'My God - he's got to be dead.'

Smithy produced the magic sponge and smelling salts, and administered both in large doses.

Eventually, Frank rose shakily to his feet, eyes rolling round in his head. Skipper Harvey pleaded: 'Howay, Norman, man, you'll have to do something to pull him around.'

A little colour seemed to be seeping back into Frank's face. Norman held up two fingers, saying: 'How many fingers, Frank? How many fingers have I got up?' The big Scot mumbled and swayed but said nowt.

After a while Frank got a little more coherent, and the referee, eager to get the game away after such a long stoppage, waved Norman off the field. As he was runnung off, Norman turned and shouted: 'Now, whatever you do, Frank, wait a few minutes before you attempt to head the ball again.'

Frank nodded, but in Wolves' very next attack he met a vicious drive square on the forehead, and the ball flew 30 yards upfield. I just held my breath, expecting Frank to topple once again, but he just grinned as the Newcastle players looked on in astonishment.

After that we refused to be flustered by being a goal down and after a peice of pure magic by Ernie Taylor, Jackie Milburn had the simplest of tap-ins to put us on level terms.

It was now Milburn's turn to be provider when he did the donkey work and left the rest to the sweet left foot of Bobby Mitchell.

So Harvey's prediction had come true, and United were off to the FA Cup Final for the eighth time in their history.

No sooner had we trooped off the field than Stan Seymour rushed into the dressing room to congratulate us: 'You did the city of Newcastle proud today, lads. You can all relax - it's an unchanged side for Wembley.'

Dramatic minute saw Wolves out

By GEORGE FOLLOWS

Newcastle United .... 2, Wolverhampton Wanderers ... 1

IN 60 sensational seconds Wolves went sliding helter-skelter out of the Cup after they had seemed to be cruising sweetly and irresistibly towards Wembley. Two goals by Jack Milburn and Bobby Mitchell, in the 32nd and 33rd minutes, stunned them at the height of their powers.

They fought back magnificently in the last 20 minutes, but though they regained their fire and purpose they never refound their poise.

All they had to show for centre after centre and corner after corner was the mark on a post where a Hancocks shot had finished.

The victory laurels for Newcastle were the muddied foreheads of Frank Brennan and Joe Harvey, who commanded the penalty area and headed every one of those corners and centres safely away.

Little Ernie

In what was a truly great game there were bound to be many fine displays. And the biggest man of all in performance was the littlest—Ernie Taylor, Newcastle's 5ft. 4in. inside-right.

Ernie deservedly follows to Wembley his brother Eddie, last year an Amateur Cup finalist with Willington.

Wearing a multi-coloured left eye, souvenir of Saturday, he made the bullets for Milburn, Mitchell and Robledo to shoot. Had the marksmanship been better there would have been several Taylor-made goals.

Last season, when Ernie was transfer-listed at £14,000, the top bid was £8,000. Said Newcastle director Stan Seymour last night: "There isn't enough money in Soccer to buy him now."

DETERMINATION: This was how Milburn looked as he drove the ball past Williams for the first of United's two-goals-in-a-minute flourish

This was how the semi-final replay was reported the next day.

It was incredible that Seymour had promised all those who played in the semi that their place was secure for the Final. There were still *six* weeks to go before Wembley. We only had to win half the nine games left and we could have done the double. But we stumbled from one league defeat to the next, including the game above against Liverpool.

There was plenty to discuss both on and off the pitch as we prepared for the FA Cup Final in April, 1951. Stan Seymour put a lot of faith in Jack Milburn getting among the goals; and skipper Joe Harvey obviously hoped that some of JET's blistering speed would rub off on him.

Back in the 1940s, Manchester United were not the force to be reckoned with that they are today. But tussles with the likes of John Downie meant that every game was fiecely contested.

From the ground, Cowell, of Newcastle, tackles Parsons, of Chelsea (left), who scrapes clear of danger.

One of the great things about keeping a scrapbook, is that you can always have a good laugh about the way you were perceived in the early days. And spot the big names in United's Reserve team: that's Ernie Taylor and Roy Bentley in the front row.

There were some fairly unorthodox methods of training at St James' Park in the 1940s.
Not that the players used to *skip* training like Milburn and Brennan in our photo.

Jack Milburn met his wife-to-be while the team were staying in a Luton
hotel. Jack is seen here with Laura and wee Ernie sporting a black eye.
Young Bob Stokoe is in th background

TOP: The 1951 Newcastle FA Cup team relax before leaving their Buxton hotel. Well, not quite the whole team - Jack Fairbrother is not in photo!
BTM shows Jackie Milburn pulling on his No 9 shirt in the Wembley dressing room prior to the Final. Note his pullover and shirt, hanging on the peg like an invisible man.

The proudest moment of any footballer's life is when he is presented to his King at an
FA Cup Final - especially if he ends up on the winning side!

BLACKPOOL F.C., 1950-51

Back Row—standing (*left to right*) E. SHIMWELL, E. HAYWARD, H. JOHNSTON (*Capt.*), G FARM, T. GARRETT, H. KELLY, A. BROWN
Front Row (*left to right*) S. MATTHEWS, W. PERRY A. WITHERS, S. MORTENSEN, J. MUDIE, R. ADAMS

Everyone said it would be 'Matthews' Final', but we proved too strong
for this Blackpool squad

That's me above on the right with Ida Harvey, next my wife Ruth and Joe Harvey at a darts presentation. Below right - Ruth and I relax after the Final at the Savoy Hotel in London.

PLAYERS' WIVES

There was just as much drama off the field as on it in 1951. Just before the squad left for Buxton to stay overnight, Ida Harvey, Joe's wife, noticed that the ticket she had been allocated for Wembley was for standing on one of the terraces.

On checking with other spouses it was found that, indeed, *all* the players' wives would have to stand. Ida, when roused, could be just as formidable an adversary as her former sergeant major husband, and she demanded that Joe, as skipper, should sort things out. No seat - no Wembley!

Joe took me and Bobby Cowell along for support when he approached Stan Seymour with the ultimatum. Seymour, said that the ticket allocation was an error, and the wives were given seats, two rows behind the Royal Box!

CAMERA ENDS THE ARGUMENT

STAN BELL SUMS UP

Many people thought that Milburn's first goal in that 1951 Final was offside. Well, now we can refute that once and for all. It is clear that when George Robledo passed the ball, Jackie was a yard *onside*.
Our reporter 'friend' Stan Bell sums up the game which gave me my first FA Cup-winners medal.

Twelve thousand "Geordies," who travelled to London with Wembley tickets, are homeward bound tonight singing the song of victory, for Newcastle were worthy conquerors over Blackpool and return next Thursday with the Cup, a proud and glorious team.

After being baffled by the offside trap in the opening half United found the complete answer in the second half by football of the highest standard. Every man in the Newcastle side deserves a pat on the back but I know they will not begrudge an extra bouquet for Jackie Milburn, the man of the match. Had he scored a third time for his "hat trick" it would have been justified. A magnificent show and tonight there will be great rejoicing.

Harvey, after the presentation, was brought onto the ground with his team holding the Cup and the ball. There was pandemonium from the "Geordie" crowd who stayed to see this grand finale to a grand final. Taylor was magnificent too, and helped Jackie to get his two successes.

Skipper Joe Harvey holds tight on the "swag" for...

IT'S NEWCASTLE'S CUP AGAIN

So the F.A. Cup goes to Newcastle again. The United defeated Blackpool in the Wembley Final by two goals to nil.

And most bitterly-disappointed footballer in the world is Stanley Matthews, who for the second time in four years had come so near and yet failed to gain a Cup-winner's medal. He had played a glorious game.

Jackie Milburn was Newcastle's particular hero for he scored the two magnificent goals that took the Cup there for the fourth time.

Full stories and pictures on the Back Page.

Initial play, as you would expect in such an important game, was scrappy. Matthews was the target for all of Blackpool's passes. In one sharp burst he went past three of us before pinpointing a cross to Bill Slater, the amateur international, but his hurried first-time shot was inches the wrong side (for him) of the post,

The two Blackpool fullbacks, Shimwell and Garrett, were man-marking Walker and Mitchell. This ploy worked in the first half and we were caught offside a few times.

The half-time whistle went with Blackpool still looking like the team to bet on. But five minutes after the re-start we were a goal up, thanks to a Jackie Milburn solo run. Robledo came out of a tackle with the ball, looked up, saw Jackie in acres of space and the rest as they say is history.

Jackie's second, thanks to a cheeky Taylor back-heel, clinched it for United, and as the final whistle blew and we claimed the Cup, Harvey was hoisted shoulder high. What a day that was!

Jackie Milburn knew that he owed that second goal to the wee fella and the wink and firm handshake in the above photo says it all.

Joe Harvey searches the crowd for signs of wor Ida; Tom Walker looks admiringly at wor Jackie while I just scrape into the frame on the right.

Not normally given to long speeches, this is how Ernie Taylor described his part in the second goal to the waiting press:

"When I got the ball from Tommy Walker, I was wondering whether to try a shot or not. But out of the corner of my eye I saw a black and white shirt streaking along. I knew that only Milburn could move like that, so I decided on a back-heel."

FIRST UNITED FANS TO GET BACK TO TYNESIDE

Although most United fans travelled by coach, a group of Ashington businessmen got together and hired a twin-engined Dakota; first off the plane back at Woolsington Airport was Bob Cooper.

THE CUP COMES HOME. "Skipper" Joe Harvey, followed by Jackie Milburn and Charlie Crowe, enters the playing pitch carrying the F.A. Cup. A tremendous welcome greeted the team as they paraded around the track at St. James's Park

After scoring his two great goals, Jackie was a natural to endorse any kind of product.

GEORGE ROBLEDO was only nineteen when he played for Barnsley against us in the FA Cup in 1945. In 1949 he joined United.

He was the perfect foil for Jackie Milburn, in fact, the Magpies had to be one of the first outfits to play with twin strikers,

George and I became good friends and often enjoyed a game of cards to while away the time on long train journeys, as above.

But he did have a temper. I can still see him voicing his displeasure to Stan Seymour after the 1951 presentation to the players at St James' Park.

We had arrived at the ground after a rapturous reception at the Central Station. Seymour wanted the players to walk around the ground in a lap of honour after meeting dignitaries.

George refused to do it at first, saying: 'Why is it at the reception the room is full of strangers? Why is that when you have refused to let my mother be present, eh?'

The year before, George had represented his country, Chile, in the World Cup Finals in Rio. He scored 91 goals for United,, playing in 164 games. He died in Vina Del Mar in 1989.

NEWCASTLE UNITED F.C. 1946-7

BACK ROW: F.G. WATT (SECT), HARVEY J., CRAIG B., GARBUT E., CORBETT R., WRIGHT W., N. SMITH (TRAINER), S. SEYMOUR (HON. MANAGER). FRONT ROW: MILBURN J., WOODBURN J., KING G., WAYMAN C., PEARSON T., BRENNAN F.

NEWCASTLE UNITED A.F.C. CUP FINALISTS, 1950-51
R. Cowell, J. Harvey (Capt.), F. Brennan, J. Fairbrother, R. Corbett, C. Crowe,
T. Walker, E. Taylor, J. Milburn, G. Robledo, R. Mitchell.

Quite a difference in Newcastle line-ups in only five short years

'PLAYED BETTER THAN YOU'

In these days of astronomical wages for footballers when it is said that some are on over £40,000 a week, it is a sobering thought to remember those so-called 'Glory Days' of Newcastle United in the 1950s.

I was telling an audience what a pittance the United players received for winning that 1951 FA Cup Final, and comparing it with what was paid to the Coldstream Guards Band who played before the match at Wembley that year.

A joker piped up: 'Aye, whey, they must have played better than you, Charlie!'

'STOT' THE BALL'

I had obtained my FA Coaching Certificate in 1950 under the then England coach, Walter Winterbottom.

After congratulating me on passing, Walter took me to one side and said: 'There is just one thing puzzles me, Charles. Could you tell me what the word 'stot' means?'

'It's a slang Geordie word for *bounce,* Walter.'

'Oh ... I see.'

Walter often talked of his vision of football in the future, saying it would be more like American football in as much as players could be substituted at any time with any given number. He also said that his ideal team would consist of ball-players in defence. In other words, everyone interchangeable. Now his ideas don't seem so far-fetched, eh!

One day on a 1951 coaching course I attended, Walter's particular theme was 'pre-match warm-ups'. He said: 'Get the team to take five balls out, three with the forwards for shooting practice to give the goalkeeper plenty of action, and one for the full-backs to hit long balls at each other, and the other for the half-backs to play short, sharp passing movements. All this to take place ten minutes before the kick-off.'

Gibby McKenzie, the manager of Scunthorpe, was attending the course. He rose to his feet as Walter finished talking, saying: 'That's all very well, Walter. But *five* balls to practise with? Man, do you not know that we only have three balls at Scunthorpe altogether, and one of them is the match ball which is washed after every home match and put away in the cupboard ready for the next home game.'

Coaching courses normally lasted a week, at the end of which there was a kick-about between the staff coaches and the course members.

After one such game, Walter made a point of telling me that he thought me a little stereotyped the way I kept hitting balls to the left-winger.

'I do that, Walter,' I said, 'because that is the general pattern of play at Newcastle United. We use the double centre-forward plan with Robledo and Milburn; the link with the forwards is through Mitchell our left-winger, and Ernie Taylor, the inside-right.

'When we attack down the left, George Robledo, who is good in the air, makes tracks for the far post to await the final cross from Mitch. An alterative approach is though Taylor, our midfield general who is always available to invite service.

'In Ernie Taylor and Bobby Mitchell we have two masters of the open space. Taylor on the right flank utilises the speed of Tommy Walker, our right-winger; and also bangs through balls for Jackie Milburn to chase.'

I think Walter accepted my explanation.

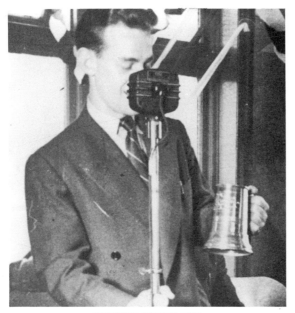

ERNIE TAYLOR

A rare shot of Ernie above for once not letting his feet do the talking. But he had plenty to say before a match at West Bromwich Albion when manager George Martin told him that six-foot plus Ray Barlow would be marking him.

'Ernie, I want you to stay with Barlow at every opportunity,' said Martin. 'I want you to harry him, stop him coming through with the ball.'

'In other words, George, you want me to mark him.'

The manager nodded.

'No chance,' replied Ernie. 'Barlow won't have any strength left after chasing *me*.'

In my early days at Newcastle, I was part of a group of players nickname *'The Clique'*. They were Tommy Walker, George Stobbart, Ernie Taylor and myself - all local lads.

During a training session, we were lapping around the ground, talking away, as young players do. Ernie was quiet which was unusual.

George said to him: "What is wrong, little'un?' (Ernie was 5ft 4ins in his stocking feet).

He replied: 'Oh, I was late getting home last night, and so the wife is not speaking to me.'

After a slight pause, George replied: 'What did she do, Ernie - put your supper in the middle of the table so you couldn't reach it?'

Jackie Milburn had just returned to the side after being on duty for England in 1950. We were playing at home and in the first half Jackie had tried to dummy his way past two defenders without much success.

In the dressing room at half-time, Ernie Taylor sidled across to where Jackie was sitting with his cup o' het waata. 'Hey, Jackie, who do you think you are, trying to dummy players? Just leave the clever stuff to me from now on, eh.'

We all smiled, including Jackie who always said that it was because of Ernie that he got into the England team in the first place.

At the start of the 1951/52 season, we were due to play in a pre-season Anglo/Scots tournament with the first game against Glasgow Celtic. It was a highly prestigious game and all the team wanted to play, especially as it was to be a good pay-day as well.

But when the teamsheet went up there was no place for myself, Bob Corbett and, amazingly, Ernie Taylor who immediately banged in a transfer request.

When Joe Harvey heard that the little man might be leaving he pleaded with Stan Seymour: 'Stan, for God's sake, don't give the wee fella a transfer. Transfer me! Anybody! But keep Ernie - he makes the whole team play.'

A month later, Ernie joined Blackpool for £25,000. The whole Newcastle team suffered.

Manchester United's No 9 in this 1956 game at Old Trafford was the late Tommy Taylor, one of the Busby Babes tragically killed in the Munich Air Disaster of 1958

We didn't need green grass in order to play a good game of football in those days.
Keeping their eye on the ball, left Crowe, McMichael, Walker and Bill Foulkes.
Apparently this was the first table-football game introduced in the UK.

'DO YE KEN HUGHIE GALLACHER?'

My first experience of Hughie was when playing against him when he played for *Huwoods*, a Gateshead factory team. He was then in his mid-forties and I found myself in the Newcastle B team who played in one of the minor leagues.

My father was a good judge of football, and he was Hughie's No 1 fan when he terrorised first division defences in the late 1920s. He had won a medal when United won the championship in 1927.

Dad often told me stories about the tricks he performed. But after the game with *Huwoods* I thought my father had understated his talents. Although slowed by age, he simply oozed class. What a player he must have been in his prime.

Hughie was transferred to Chelsea, and when he returned to play for the Londoners against the Magpies it resulted in Newcastle's biggest ever gate at St James' Park, 68,586, which stands to this day and I can't see it being beaten.

During Hughie's reign as the king of Gallowgate, the fans used to sing about him, much the same way they did with Andy Cole in the early Nineties. Set to the music of *John Peel*, Hughie's anthem went:

Do ye ken Hughie Gallacher the wee Scotch lad
The best centre-forward Newcastle ever had
If he doesn't score a goal, sign him on the dole
And send him back to Scotland in the morning.

In 1990 during Mike Kirkup's musical 'Wor Jackie', one of the characters sings about Hughie

When he gets the ball, defenders quake and quiver
They're convinced this man turns water into wine
And when he hits the net he sets the spines a'shiverin'
From Glasgow to Newcastle on Tyne.

That's Hughie second left with his pals at the Pelaw Social Club when I took the 1951 FA Cup for the lads to sup from.

'WHAT'S THE SCORE?'

In the run-up to an important game, I was visited by a happy event. By then Ruth and I were the parents of two beautiful girls, Cathy having arrived in 1950 to keep Lesley company.

We were staying at a Blackpool hotel prior to going over to play Manchester United. Staying at the same hotel was a pal of Alec Mutch, our physio: the great comedian Jimmy James who was playing the Winter Gardens.

I knew that Ruth was expecting at any time, but because we were not on the phone at home, getting information was proving difficult. Let Ruth take up the story:

'The birth went OK with one boy being born, but ten minutes later I became the mother of twins - *two* boys!

'I was visited by Alec Mutch's wife and I asked if she would ring the hotel from her phone to pass on the message to Charlie, which she did.'

Ah, yes, but ... . When the phone rang we were all in the lounge in a large company which included this Jimmy James. Alec took the call and when he came back into the room, his face beaming, he said: 'Congratulations, Charlie, you're the father of twins!'

'Oh, aye,' I said, 'come on, what's the score?'

'Charlie, I am not having you on, lad ... your Ruth has just given birth to twin laddies.'

At which point Jimmy James chirped up: 'Well, my son, you'll not be the only chap who's come to Blackpool with two kids and gone away the father of four!'

(That's the complete family above).

'I WILL STAY'

The season after winning that first FA Cup, Stan Seymour began to dismantle the team. The first to go was Bobby Corbett, transferred to Middlesbrough - he hadn't even asked for a move. Alf McMichael took over at left-back. Ernie Taylor was dropped from the team, replaced by George Hannah; wee Ernie asked for a move and he joined Blackpool. Ronnie Simpson took over in goal from Jack Fairbrother. I, myself, was dropped and young Ted Robledo stepped in.

New players seemed to be arriving on practically every train that stopped at Newcastle Central: Bill Foulkes, Reg Davies, Tommy Cahill, Johnny Duncan, Tom Mulgrew and George Brander.

I was disenchanted by the events and after long deliberations asked for a transfer in December, 1951. Stan Seymour refused to let me go - he insisted I had been 'nobbled', that is approached by another team. The Press said I had started a new fashion by lobbying each director in turn to plead my case. I called to see Seymour nearly every day. But his reply was always: 'You are not leaving and that's final.' There were occasions when he would not look me in the face, often turning in his swivel chair to face the wall.

After a wasted season and about six weeks before our second FA Cup Final against Arsenal, Stan call me in for a talk: 'Charlie,' he said, ''if you change your mind about wanting to leave you may have a chance of playing in the final at Wembley. And another thing, you will also receive the same cup-final tickets as the rest of the team. And you will be included in the party to tour South Africa for ten weeks after the Final. I will give you twenty-four hours to think it over.'

'No need,' I replied, quickly, 'I will stay.'

1952 FA CUP FINAL

As in the previous year, United decided to make the Royal Albion Hotel in Brighton their base before the final. The planned leisure activity for the squad was Monday and Tuesday free; Wednesday golf at Roehampton; Thursday see ice-hockey game; Friday go to the theatre.

While the lads were in Brighton for the week, back home in Newcastle some of Stan Seymour's thoughts were appearing in the *Journal:*

'When I was a player, I constantly looked to the future. I rented two little shops and sold cigarettes and confectionery, later switching to sports outfitters. I can only speak for myself, but I do not think the United board would raise the slightest objection to any player, even today, doing the same as I did, so long as he is his own master and gives his full time to all calls made upon him by the club.'

This was a direct indication that Newcatle players could, from that moment, take part-time employment which I and several others did

The final turned out to be a dour match. Jack Milburn, writing in his newspaper column, said: 'From the moment Wally Barnes was injured until the end of the match, the Londoners kept themselves in the game. There was even a lack of drama about the goal which won the match. Mitchell put over a centre, and it seemed a lifetime as Robledo's header floated slowly through the air, hit an upright, and glided over the line.

'There was a tremendous roar of excitement from the Geordies in the crowd. Yet there was none of the tension, and I for one did not feel the satisfaction of the previous year.'

Frank Brennan agreed: 'It was nothing like the first time. Nothing ever is. First time is always the best.'

There was no place for me in the
1952 FA Cup Final against Arsenal.

Milburn, of Newcastle, gets the ball away from Daniel, Arsenal centre half, near Arsenal's goal.

The ball goes over the line to beat Swindin. And dark little George Robledo has scored.

Two incidents from a drab cup final.

SOUTH AFRICA TOUR, 1952

On May 11th, 1952, the first of the United party left for South Africa on the Pullman train *Northumbrian*. We didn't know it then, but it was the start of journey that would take us 20,000 miles, more than three-quarters of which were by air.

For safety reasons the team travelled in two groups, the first being made up of directors Seymour and Taylor, together with Harvey, Simpson, Cowell, Walker, Davies, Foulkes and Mitchell; this group was joined in London by Ted Robledo who was on holiday there at the time.

As the train pulled away from the Central Station, Joe Harvey waved and shouted: 'We hope to do Newcastle credit.' Stan Seymour told the press: 'We want to show the South Africans what a grand game football is.'

The second group included myself, Lord Westwood, Norman Smith, McMichael, Batty, Brennan, Milburn, George Robledo, Hannah, and Bob Stokoe. Typically, just before the train was due to leave, Frank still had not arrived. Norman Smith was looking everywhere for him. He spotted big Frank entering the station, dressed in his new lightweight suit, but without luggage.

'Where's all your stuff, Frank?' he asked.

Frank tapped his breast pocket out of which stuck a toothbrush. 'I didna forget it, Norman - it's all here.'

The tour proved to be a tiring one for everybody. With only half of the games played, of the sixteen players we had in the party only Joe Harvey had played every game.

Seymour and Norman Smith called a meeting with the players to suggest a team for the next game. Our biggest problem was that we had Milburn and Robledo both unfit with no adequate cover up front. Frank Brennan, who always fancied himself as a striker, persuaded Stan Seymour to play him at centre-forward, so Stan pencilled him in.

Going up in the lift to our hotel bedrooms, Frank was full of it and going on about how many goals he would score. I tried to bring him down to earth: 'Frank, you know, you are *not* the most skillful player in the world, and even your best friend would never say you were constructive with your passes.'

The big'un lifted me off my feet and growled: 'What did ye say?'

But Frank did score and had the last laugh when we beat Northern Rhodesia 6-1. And even *I* scored in that game as well as Joe Harvey ... *and* ace defender Bobby Cowell.

Due to the bone hard pitches in South Africa, our ball-players such as Mitchell and Hannah found the ball almost impossible to control. It was like playing on concrete, with the ball bouncing all over the stadium.

We played Johannesburgh in what was billed as football's first Test Match. It was still goal-less at half-time when the teams broke for a 15-minute interval. The dressing rooms were quite some distance from the pitch so they had put some wooden benches on the touchline for us to sit, suck an orange and have a soft drink. There was also a couple of buckets of water for our use.

Unseen by anyone, big Frank put the match ball in the bucket of water, then Milburn sat on it!

As the second half got under way it was noticeable that the home team had great difficulty with the now much heavier ball, soaked through with water while our play improved.

But alas our ploy failed and we lost our only game of the tour 5-3.

A banner headline in the *Rand Daily* next day screamed out: '*Go Home Newcastle - Cheating Cup Holders.*'

We usually played cricket in the summer, but in 1952 found ouselves flying
to South Africa.

A SUPERSTITIOUS IRISHMAN

One of the games was against Lourenco Marques, a Portugese outfit. We travelled there from Pretoria via the Kruger National Park, the largest game reserve of animals in the world. The South Africa FA had hired a fleet of cars and guards to get us overland. Our first stop was at Komatipoort, a clearing surrounded by high fencing. A huge bonfire was lit in the centre which burned all night

We slept in single beds set up in a kraal in which was a small table and an oil-lamp. The kraal's also had two flimsy doors, constructed with mosquito netting. We had been on the road for twelve hours and were exhausted.

After supper in a wooden hut, we talked to the four huge negroes who were acting as our guards. They told us many stories of lions and other wild beasts leaping over the stockade and prowling around.

I was rooming with Alf McMichael, a superstitious Irishman. I dropped off to an uneasy sleep and was awakened by Alf trying to light the oil-lamp. He whispered: 'Listen. Can you hear that?' Even though I was half asleep I could indeed hear moans and groans, grunts and scratching at the bamboo door.

'Come on, Charlie ... we're running away from here.'

'Run where to, Alf? There's nowhere to go.'

'I'm seeing Seymour tomorrow,' cried Alf. 'And I am flying home. I have had enough'

I managed to get Alf calmed down and we both dozed into a fitful sleep. Alf told his story to Seymour and Smith in the morning. When he left they burst out laughing. It transpired that *they* had been the wild animals.

When we arrived at our destination, the home team supporters were offering the generous odds of three to one against Newcastle beating their pride and joy.

The home goalie was Costa Perreira, a snazzy dresser in striped blue shorts, yellow jersey, two caps - one for wearing and one for waving to the crowd who game him a tremendous ovation as he swaggered on to the pitch.

Five minutes into the game, he misjudged a cross and handled the ball outside the penalty area. The ref award a direct free kick. Costa handed me the ball as if he was making a presentation, turned around and trotted back to his goal, waving his second cap to the crowd.

As I put the ball down ready to take the free kick, Mitch, who was standing next to me, shouted: 'Now, Charlie!' So I sidefooted the ball the ball to Bob who blasted the ball into the net, past the startled Perreira who was still headed back to his goal.

He was furious, but not half as mad as when we scored another two goals to lead 3-0 after only thirteen minutes.

Perreira seemed to think it was his yellow jersey that was bringing him bad luck so he threw it into the back of the net and proceded to play in his vest for the rest of the game.

But after our third goal went in, his fan club began to desert him. Every time the ball went anywhere near the home goalposts, the hapless custodian was barracked with catcalls, blowing whistles and the waving of handkerchiefs.

The rout of the Portugese was now completed and the big crowd watched the rest of the game in hushed silence as though mourners at a very sad funeral.

The phrase *Howay the Black & Whites* took on a competely new
meaning in Durban for players Robledo, McMichael, Crowe,
Milburn, Foulkes and Brennan.

TIRED, HOMESICK UNITED BACK

NEWCASTLE UNITED tourists are home again. The final party touched down at London Airport yesterday, having travelled by Comet jet air liner from Johannesburg.

Aboard were Milburn, Brennan, Hannah, McMichael, George Robledo, Crowe, Stokoe, Batty and trainer Norman Smith. They arrived by train at Newcastle last night.

Earlier, by Constellation plane, had come Harvey, Mitchell, Walker, Ted Robledo, Cowell, Simpson, Davies and Foulkes.

RECUPERATING

All are fit and well and today they are recuperating from an "epidemic"—home-sickness.

Every man expressed the same view—the tour was far too lengthy, too much travelling and too much football.

Since leaving home in May the team have travelled by land and air over 21,000 miles, played sixteen games and won fifteen.

All expenses were paid by the South African F.A., with a £2-a-day spending money allowance and no final profit for the club.

ORDEALS

Check-up last night brought the following opinions on the success of the tour:—

Joe Harvey: The unending travelling, the hard grounds and the atmospherical conditions were ordeals and I, for one, am glad it is all over. We should have played fewer games and we should have made Johannesburg the base instead of being hawked around South Africa non-stop.

Jackie Milburn: Hectic is the word. I only played five games but, like the rest of the lads, it was a joy to put a foot down once again on English soil. It was too big a programme for any team to undertake.

Frank Brennan: A wonder tour, but there's no place like home.

Tommy Walker: Never again for me. Apart from the non-Europeans, the crowds were anything but sporting. I've had all the holidays I want for a long time.

Ted Robledo: It was an experience, but it is grand to be home again. I think we were all tired of it long before the final game. The itinerary was too big to undertake.

Mrs. Tommy Walker: We don't see much of our men during the season. To take them away for the summer is cruel. The directors must think we don't like them. Close season tours are no good to the footballers' wives.

VIC KEEBLE, 1952 - 57

When Vic arrived at Newcastle from Colchester, supposedly to take over from Jackie Milburn, he told a sports' reporter that he would try 'To make the Geordie supporters forget all about wor Jackie.' For all that, he was a likeable man and his words had been taken out of context. But it did not endear him to the Newcastle faithful to whom Jackie had become a living legend.

With the ball at his feet, Keeble looked decidedly clumsy, but in the air he was quite majestic. In one game he scored a hat-trick. After the first goal the fans chanted 'KEEEEBLE'; after the second it was 'VIIIICK'; but the third was greeted with VIIIICTOR'.

The lads on the team called him '*The Camel*' and the fans would swear that one day Vic would take a penalty kick with his head. In all, he played 120 games for United, scoring 67 goals.

I was on a coaching course during the summer of 1953 with Mickey Fenton, 'Boro's England centre-forward. Next season we played at Ayresome Park in a league match against the 'Boro. I always made a habit of leaving the dressing room last. And as we trooped on to the field Micky stopped me: 'Hey, Charlie, who the hell is that new number 9 of yours?'

'Oh, that's Vic Keeble. How's that, like?'

'Whey, man, what a funny shape he is. I bet you couldn't bend a piece o' wire his shape.'

During a home match with Manchester City, Vic was opposed by a rugged centre-half called Dave Ewing. I had been involved in a tussle and came out of it hurting in a very delicate place.

'Do a few exercises, Charlie,' said Norman Smith, 'then you can get back on to the pitch.'

As I got up from the bench, Ewing and Keeble both went up for a high ball. They clashed heavily and Vic fell to the ground and stayed there, motionless.

Norman had finished with me and grabbed the water sponge and bag while waiting for the ref's signal to come on the pitch to attend to Keeble. At that moment a voice from the Paddock enclosure rang out: 'Leave him alone, Norman. With a bit of luck he might die.'

I turned to face the fan with the loud voice thinking he was having a bit of a joke, but I could see by his face that he had meant every word.

SUNDERLAND V ARSENAL, 1952

Roker Park was a mudbath and incessant rain had made the game something of a lottery. Billy Bingham, Sunderland's Irish international winger, had skirmishes with Arsenal's Forbes and Smith, scrambling for the ball.

Within seconds the trio were covered in mud from top to toe. Eventually, Bingham got the ball away from the Arsenal defenders, reached the bye-line and crossed to the far post. George Swindon, Arsenal's goalie, came for it, but completely misjudged the flight of the ball which sailed over his head to Len Shackleton standing alone.

Anyone else but Len would have whacked it straight into the empty net, saying thank you very much. Not so Len He stood with the ball at his feet and shouted out to Bingham: 'Come on, Billy, you've done all the hard work. Come and put it in.'

Acccording to Joe Mercer the Arsenal skipper, time seemed to stand still as he and a couple of defenders threw themselves at Shack. But Len casually tapped the ball over the line then trotted back to the half-way line.

Who on earth could do a thing like that but Len Shackleton, Clown Prince of Soccer?

WOLVES V NEWCASTLE, 1953

We were relaxing in the lounge of our hotel on the Friday evening before the match. George Hannah was reading the local paper when he spotted a preview of the game.

'Hey, Bobby, here's a piece of news that should interest you.'

'Gan on then, read it out,' said Bob Cowell.

'Well, there's a big headline here which says 'Blow for Wolves - Mullen out of tomorrow's big game.'

Now the reason that *that* was good news for Bobby was because he and the Wolves and England international left-winger had had some rare tussles over the previous years. So as far as Bobby was concerned that was good news,

But Mullen's stand-in was a lad called Denis Wilshaw who scored a hat-trick against us the next day. Wolves won easily and Mullen's deputy was the star player. Bobby was as sick as a parrot. Wilshaw was later capped for England.

BOLTON V NEWCASTLE, 1953

On a bone-hard pitch at Burnden Park with sub-zero temperature, one incident stood out showing the power and strength of Nat Lofthouse, the England centre-forward. Bolton's right-half Wheeler made progress down the right side of the field and attempted a crossfield pass to the left-winger. But he mis-hit the ball which screamed across the field chest high to Nat who was closely marked by Frank Brennan.

Lofthouse had no room to manouevre the ball, but he turned half to the right and *chested* the ball fully twenty yards to Holden on the wing. Joe Harvey and I looked at each other. Nat smiled, lifted up his shirt showing the panel marks of the ball embedded into his chest. He was not named the *Lion of Vienna* for nothing!

MAN UTD RES V NEWCASTLE RES

It was during this game that I got my first glimpse of 'Big Dunc' - Duncan Edwards the Red Devils' left-half.

George Robledo and I had been dropped from the first team. The inside forward playing directly against me was Roger Byrne who later captained the Busby Babes.

Old Trafford was heavy that day and Robledo and Edwards were giving no quarter nor expecting any. George was a husky Chilean international who was not easily intimidated.

Just before half-time, the pair clashed in a tackle which echoed all around the ground. After that tackle, Roger turned to me and said: 'Do you know how old that lad is, Charlie?'

I shook my head.

'He's only fifteen years of age!'

I could not believe it. Two years later Duncan was capped for England, making him one of the youngest players ever to represent his country. Sadly, he died in hospital after the 1958 Munich air disaster.

BILL PATERSON, 1954

Bill had been signed to be a replacement for Frank Brennan. He made his debut against Spurs in a game which ended in a 4-4 draw. He played a sweeper-type role in defence which was not a success. Jimmy Scoular, Tom Casey and myself all agreed that Bill Paterson in the middle of our defence would shorten our footballing careers by at least three years!

Robin Lawlor, an Irish international, watching a United match in which Paterson was giving a particularly inept performance, asked how much we had paid for him. When told the price, he said: 'Indeed to goodness, it's the biggest robbery since the Crown Jewels.'

CARTOONIST DUDLEY HALLWOOD also saw the funny side of the Newcastle United–Spurs match at St. James's Park on Saturday.

Everyone had a laugh at Bill Paterson's expense
in the 4-4 draw with Spurs,
PS Even *I* managed to get my name on the scoresheet.

'I'LL GET HIM IN MY OWN TIME'

In 1954, Joe Harvey had become club coach once Bob Stokoe had established himself as United's first team choice. We were playing away against Bolton and I was selected by the players to be captain of United, an honour which I always treasured.

In one of Bolton's early attacks, their captain, Billy Moir, who also played for Scotland, had made a few late tackles on Ronnie Simpson in our goal. Ron asked me if there was anything I could do to sort him out.

'Not to worry, Ron,' I said, 'I'll get him in my own time.' But the opportunity never came my way until late in the second half - by then we were leading 1-0.

Ron came out for a cross with Moir and myself in close attendance. He caught the ball and threw it straight to Jimmy Scoular on the right. Jimmy made ground and fed a perfect ball to Mitchell who crossed for Keeble to head just over the bar.

That's when I hit Billy Moir! But when I turned round, there was the small, portly referee who whistled and pointed to the spot, awarding Bolton a penalty.

I was annoyed and shouted at him: 'Hey, you should have been up with the play,' but he didn't answer.

Moir picked himself up and handed the ball to Harold Hassall, saying to me: 'He will not miss.'

And Hassall did blast the ball past Ronnie Simpson, giving him no chance and levelling the scores at 1-1 which ultimately was the fnal result.

After the game all the talk was about the penalty incident which the majority of the crowd never saw. Stan Seymour and Joe Harvey were never off my back. Not because they had not *seen* the incident, but that I should concede a penalty at such a late stage in the game.

DOUGALD LIVINGSTONE, 1954/55

On December 9th, 1954, the Newcastle board, on the instructions of Stan Seymour who had been virtually running the team since 1949, decided to appoint a manager: Dougald Livingstone, a dour Scot, who had been coaching in Belgium. His brief was 'Confined to coaching, supervision of training, and all matters pertaining to play'. Joe Harvey was to stay on as coach with Norman Smith as trainer.

After a gap of two years we were on the Wembley trail again with a third-round draw against Plymouth. But I sustained an ankle injury and lost my place as left-half and captain.

Livingstone's ideas of training and tactical talks often left us seasoned performers cold. During one pre-match talk Doug said to me: 'Charlie, I want you to vary your service to Mitch by hitting balls which will bisect their full-backs and the corner flag for Mitch to chase.' While this was being said Bobby Mitchell was being ominously silent.

As we were running on to the field, Bob said: 'If you do that to me, Charlie, I will not run after the ball.'

I knew the canny Scot well enough to know that he meant every word. We both played our normal game, won the match, and 'bisecting passes' were never mentioned again.

Doug introduced a form of circuit training. The format was for us to run around the perimeter at St James' jumping up and heading an imaginary ball, sprint thirty yards and finish with neck-roll, trot thirty yards, and walk thirty yards doing bend and stretch exercises, ending up sprinting fifty yards jumping over high hurdles.

While jumping a hurdle I pulled a muscle above my knee, and Ronnie Simpson sustained the same injury. We told Norman Smith who told Stan Seyour who told Doug to stop it.

One of my lasting memories: leading the lads on to St James' Park as
Newcastle United's captain.

PART-TIME JOB

Shortly before Livingstone arrived I had spoken to the then honorary manager Stan Seymour about my future and he had agreed to let me take a part-time job outside football. It was in 1954 that I joined a builders' merchant as a sales representative. This started a trend with other players doing likewise such as Ron Simpson, Bob Mitchell and Jack Milburn who advertised for a shoe manufacture.

THE REVIE PLAN

After Puskas and his fellow Hungarians had destroyed England in 1953 with the deep-lying centre-forward system, it was adopted by Manchester City and brought success to the club and its main architect Don Revie. But when we played Man City our tactics were simple: the nearest player always took on Revie, and that way no one was drawn out of position. My own view, however, is that he should have had a specialised marker.

IVOR BROADIS, 1953/55

Ivor Broadis and Jimmy Scoular were never the best of friends during Ivor's two-year stint at Newcastle. He was once chided for his lack of hair and replied: 'I played two years in front of Jimmy Scoular - that would make anyone lose his hair.'

I was walking to the ground one day for morning training. It was belting down with rain and as we entered the car-park a brand-new car came hurtling towards us tooting its horn. It was Ivor at the wheel. Scoular gave Ivor a mouthful in the dressing room. Ivor replied: 'Sorry James but if you would like to relieve your feelings, feel free to urinate on my car bonnet.'

Newcastle United stumbled through the early rounds of the FA Cup and before we knew it we were Wembley bound again. Three years out of five must surely be a record that will never be beaten!

But, true to form, Newcastle United were making a pig's ear of their arrangements in the run-up to the final. Three weeks before the final there were still some pertinent questions left unanswered. For instance, who, out of a first-team squad of fifteen players, would get the nod for Wembley? Would the players get the usual 100 cup-final tickets to dispose of as they wished? And what arrangements had been made for players' wives to obtain seats at Wembley?

The players held a meeting and chose three to put those questions to the management: Scoular. Broadis and myself. After our meeting with the board we had assurances on tickets and seats for the wives. The vexed question of team selection had not been resolved.

When we conveyed the news to the rest of the squad they were still not happy, but none more so than Ivor Broadis who had been particularly quiet during our meeting with the bosses.

"I know *one* player who won't be in the line-up on cup-final day.'

'Who is that, Ivor?' was the question on everyone's lips.

'Well, *me* for a start! When we were in the room I stood behind the club secretary, Ted Hall. When someone was talking I looked at the papers on Ted's desk. On one sheet was a list of names with my name *top* of the list.'

'But surely that means that you are one of the bankers for the big game?' someone asked.

'No fear! The heading at the top of the page read: *'Open for Transfer'*. I'm on my way, lads!' With that, Ivor left the room.

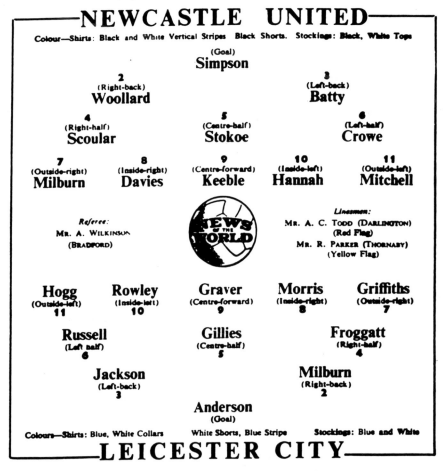

SATURDAY 5th FEBRUARY, 1955

KICK-OFF 3 p.m.

Team changes will be announced over the loudspeakers

NEWCASTLE UNITED

Colour—Shirts: Black and White Vertical Stripes. Black Shorts. Stockings: Black, White Tops

(Goal)
Simpson

2
(Right-back)
Woollard

3
(Left-back)
Batty

4
(Right-half)
Scoular

5
(Centre-half)
Stokoe

6
(Left-half)
Crowe

7
(Outside-right)
Milburn

8
(Inside-right)
Davies

9
(Centre-forward)
Keeble

10
(Inside-left)
Hannah

11
(Outside-left)
Mitchell

Referee:
MR. A. WILKINSON
(BRADFORD)

Linesmen:
MR. A. C. TODD (DARLINGTON)
(Red Flag)
MR. R. PARKER (THORNABY)
(Yellow Flag)

Hogg
(Outside-left)
11

Rowley
(Inside-left)
10

Graver
(Centre-forward)
9

Morris
(Inside-right)
8

Griffiths
(Outside-right)
7

Russell
(Left half)
6

Gillies
(Centre-half)
5

Froggatt
(Right-half)
4

Jackson
(Left-back)
3

Milburn
(Right-back)
2

Anderson
(Goal)

Colours—Shirts: Blue, White Collars   White Shorts, Blue Stripe   Stockings: Blue and White

LEICESTER CITY

MUSIC BY PEGSWOOD COLLIERY PRIZE BAND

The Leicester right-back was Stan Milburn, cousin of Jackie and brother of Cissie Charlton.
On the opposite page is the way *Voice of United* saw our 1955 FA Cup chances.

VOICE OF UNITED

So we have to travel to Nottingham to meet the Forest in the 5th round of the F.A. Cup on February 19th, a date that postpones the St. James's Park League match arranged for that day against Cardiff City. We had hoped for a victory for Manager Fred Westgarth's team, gallant Hartlepools United, to give us a great North East Derby, but fate has decreed otherwise. Sad that Notts should gain the initiative in the replay mid-week at Nottingham through a Kelly penalty goal, and win only in extra time. The defeat of the Pools, however, has solved a problem that would have baffled the football world, for our share of tickets for a Cup game at Hartlepool would have been less than 4,000. How this distribution could have been carried out is anyone's guess.

What are United's chances of making further progress along the Wembley road? Against Second Division opposition they must be regarded as good, but we shall have to tackle the Forest with much more zest than we did Plymouth Argyle or Brentford. The door is wide open for another Wembley call if United are true to themselves. They have the talent to be finalists once again. Not for many seasons has such an opportunity knocked to gain a success in the F.A. Cup competition. Most of the top teams have been drawn together and the number greatly reduced. In having to meet Notts Forest, previous clashes in the competition can be recalled with enthusiasm, for we have met the Midlands side on three previous occasions. In 1908 in the days of Appleyard and Rutherford, we beat them at Gallowgate by two clear goals; in 1921 we "bought" them to St. James's Park after being drawn away and met them twice at St. James's to end with a 2-0 win, and then again in 1931 we met the Forest and defeated them at home by four clear goals. In the 1921 battle our chairman Mr. Stan Seymour was our winger and the winning side: Lawrence; McCracken, Hudspeth; Curry, Low Finlay; Aitken, Ward, Harris, Smailes, Seymour.

On to 1931 when we triumphed over Forest by 4-0. The team that day: McInroy; Nelson, Fairhurst; Naylor, Davidson, Weaver; Boyd, Bedford, Hutchinson, Starling, Wilkinson. Hutchinson scored a hat-trick and Bedford added another. Happy recollections indeed for the old school.

So much then for the things that are to come. How about the present? Well today we will be out to take revenge over Leicester City for they beat us in September after we had held a winning lead. Interest will be added by the appearance of former United player Andy Graver who left Lincoln City a few weeks ago for a £30,000 fee.

1955 FA CUP RUN

With the sixth-round tie with Huddersfield only days away, Livingstone was still undecided about the team's format. He told the press: 'I prefer to watch the men in training another day or two before choosing the cup team.'

We made the Norbreck Hotel at Blackpool our base before the match. It was a popular stopping over point with its facilities for the hydro and golf course. Len White, an ex-pitman, joked: 'I'm playing a better game of golf ... now that I've taken the wrapper off the ball.' The night before the game we went to Blackpool Tower to watch a boxing match.

For the crucial game at Huddersfield we again fielded a changed forward line of White, Broadis, Keeble, Milburn and Mitchell. We trailed by 1-0 until Milburn set up a goal for Len White to send yet another Newcastle cup-tie to a replay.

Extra time was needed in the replay before goals by Mitchell and Keeble made sure of that semi-final place against neighbours York City.

Again we only scraped through with a 1-1 scoreline at Hillsborough. Vic Keeble scored the all-important goal which took the tie to Roker Park where we won emphatically 2-0 with White and Keeble scoring. But there was a price to pay: Jackie Milburn - an ever-present in cup games - pulled a groin muscle and was sidelined for a fortnight.

Just over a week before the cup final, we played Tottenham at White Hart Lane. It was then the line-up for Wembley was disclosed to the press: Simpson, Cowell, Batty, Scoular, Stokoe, Crowe, Milburn, Davies, Keeble, Hannah, and Mitchell. Len White was chosen as travelling reserve.

But that didn't tell the full story. Livingstone had presented *his* team to the directors days before that. And it was a team that did not include the name of Jackie Milburn. He preferred Len White. His team selection was summarily despatched to the waste paper basket, and within forty-eight hours Livingstone was himself banished from his office into the cubby-hole set aside for match-day referees.

But the events of my own personal agony still remained to be played out. During the game with Spurs I had to be assisted from the field after falling awkwardly in a tackle with Harry Clark.

Brighton physio and masseur Sam Cowan, attached to the Sussex County Cricket Club, was enlisted to treat my badly swollen ankle. On the Wednesday before the final it was decided to send for Tom Casey to join the party at Brighton's Royal Albion Hotel, just in case my ankle did not respond to treatment.

On the Friday morning, the ankle was still very stiff and puffy. Stan Seymour asked me for a decision by mid afternoon. After turning and kicking the ball, Norman Smith said to me: It's not right, is it, Charlie?'

It was then that Jackie Milburn whispered: 'You can still play, Charlie. Me and the rest of the lads will "carry" you if you break down.'

But I knew it wasn't right, and told Seymour. Poor Reg Davies developed laryngitis so Len White was drafted in at the last minute, making the forward line read: White, Milburn, Keeble, Hannah and Mitchell.

It was a tragedy for Reg, but everyone was pleased about Len White playing against Man City in the final. It was what he deserved.

The squad was 'up for it', as they say, and Seymour told the press: 'At Wembley we will put the hat-trick seal on five wonderful years.'

The fact that Jackie Milburn went into the record books with a 45-second goal seemed more important than the actual 3-1 victory. Part of my disappointment melted away when United had a winners' medal minted especially for me.

Manager Doug Livingstone does not appear to be holding a good hand against
Bob Mitchell, myself, Bob Cowell and Ron Simpson in March, 1955.

Sam Cowan did his best to get me on the pitch at Wembley
but it was always going to be an outside chance.

It was agony sitting on the bench
and the champagne is never so
sweet out of a tea-cup

CUP SECRET IS OUT!

'Manager wanted to omit Milburn

by Edgar Turner

NEWCASTLE UNITED director Stan Seymour last night revealed to me the inside story of the rift with their ex-manager, Duggie Livingstone, whose contract was recently ended by mutual consent.

It revolved round the selection for last year's Cup Final of Jackie Milburn, the man who put United on the path to a 3—1 win over Manchester City with a goal after 45 seconds.

"Although Livingstone was normally entrusted with the task of selecting his own team, the directors, of which I was then chairman, felt the occasion was so important that we all ought to have a say," said Mr. Seymour.

"I therefore asked the board, together with the manager, to nominate their teams and, with the exception of Livingstone, we all included Milburn.

"Livingstone had left out Jackie for Len White.

'Justified'

"THE board were more than surprised. We knew all about Milburn's capacities for winning a match.

"Naturally, our confidence in Livingstone was shaken, and we relieved him of first-team management four days after the final.

"Milburn certainly fully justified to the hilt the board's faith in him."

Note: Both Newcastle and Livingstone had their way in the end. Reg Davies went down with tonsillitis and Milburn was moved to inside-right, White taking over the right-wing position.

Jackie Milburn

It was unthinkable that Newcastle could ever play in an FA Cup Final in the 1950s without Jackie Milburn. Even an out-of-form Jackie was enough to lift the team.

Livingstone leaves Newcastle—no plans for future

By Sunday Dispatch Reporter

MR. DUGALD LIVINGSTONE announced yesterday that his contract as manager-coach of Newcastle United had been cancelled, by mutual agreement. His contract still had nearly two years to run.

Before joining Newcastle—in December 1954—he had coached the successful Belgian F.A. national team for four years.

He said yesterday before leaving for his home in Sheffield : " I am no longer connected with Newcastle United.

" The real reason for the parting is that since Newcastle United won the Cup last May duties have been taken away from me until there was nothing left for me to do.

" It began four days after the Cup Final, when I was told that I would no longer select the Newcastle team.

" The records show that at that time Newcastle United had only lost six of the 28 games played during my active period in the job, and, of course, they had won the Cup.

Mr. Livingstone

'Browned off'

" But things were not going so well when I took over on January 1 last year. When I saw my team in action as manager for the first time it lost 6—2 to Sheffield United.

Mr. Raymond Hunter, chairman of the United Supporters Club said : " I suppose Livingstone became browned off. What else can you expect when a man is appointed to one job then is told he must stop doing it, until finally there is nothing left for him to do."

Doug Livingstone went the way of many Magpie managers who have stepped out of line over the years.

United will get great welcome

This one started it

ABOUT 150,000 people are expected to line Newcastle streets tomorrow night to welcome back Newcastle United with the Cup.

On their arrival the team will board an open motor coach and go to St. James's Park, where the players will march round with Scoular carrying the Cup.

The team and officials will arrive at Newcastle Central Station at 6.30 p.m. to be greeted by the Lord Mayor. They will leave the station by the side of the portico and will travel by three buses along Neville Street, Collingwood Street, Mosley Street, Grey Street, Blackett Street and Gallowgate to the Barrack Road entrance of St. James's Park.

The Cup is returning for the third time in five years. Also coming back with the team will be the lucky penny which made its fifth visit to Wembley.

HOMECOMING

It was sent by a supporter to the late Mr. Frank G. Watt, club secretary, just before the 1924 Final, and that was the start of United's Wembley successes.

It was the first television Cup Final for Newcastle as far as Tyneside was concerned, and the city streets were very quiet.

After midnight the excursion trains began to draw into Newcastle Central Station, bringing the fans back home.

There were a few who rang bells. There were some who sang. But most, looking tired but happy, just stood around talking and at last made their way home.

"Had a good day, Geordie?" shouted black-and-white muffler. "One of the best, Geordie." replied black-and-white rosette. And he was speaking for them all.

"THAT'S how I did it," says Jackie Milburn to his wife, as they study a Kemsley picture of his sensational goal at last night's Newcastle United victory banquet at the Savoy Hotel, London.

Dudley Hallwood was a great cartoonist

THEIR THIRD CUP WIN IN FIVE YEARS

By J. G. ORANGE

NEWCASTLE HAVE WON THE CUP. TO-DAY THEY ADDED TO THEIR ILLUSTRIOUS WEMBLEY RECORD WHEN THEY WON THERE FOR THE FIFTH TIME IN AS MANY VISITS.

Manchester City were fighting setbacks from the start. In a shock opening Jackie Milburn headed a goal from a corner in the first 60 seconds.

CUP FINAL LINE-UP

NEWCASTLE UTD.
(Black and white striped shirts, black shorts)

R. SIMPSON

B. COWELL   R. BATTY

J. SCOULAR   B. STOKOE   T. CASEY

J. MILBURN   G. HANNAH

L. WHITE   V. KEEBLE   B. MITCHELL

Referee: ⚫ Mr. R. Leafe (Nottingham)

P. FAGAN   D. REVIE   B. SPURDLE

B. JOHNSTONE   J. HAYES

R. PAUL   D. EWING   K. BARNES

R. LITTLE   J. MEADOWS

B. TRAUTMANN

MANCHESTER CITY
(Sky blue shirts, white shorts)

THE CUP WIVES AT THE MATCH OF THE YEAR

Off to Wembley to cheer their husbands are the wives of eight of Newcastle United's Cup Final team. Left to right: Mrs. Joyce Scoular, Mrs. Elsie Cowell, Mrs. Isobel Mitchell, Mrs. Laura Milburn, Mrs. Jean Stokoe, Mrs. Lily Batty, Mrs. June Hannah and Mrs. Joyce White.

JACKIE MILBURN, 1943-57

One of the finest sights in football was Jack in full flight chasing a through ball with his shirt billowing out behind him.

Apart from his blinding speed and shooting power, Jack had cultivated what we all thought was a bad habit which would result in him being hurt if he persisted in doing it. That was his sliding tackle where he would hook the ball away from the defender, then control the ball perfectly. While he was sliding towards the ball, his leg was competely unprotected and at risk. Yet, during his long career, he never suffered any serious injury. He had perfected the sliding tackle.

When we toured South Africa in 1952, Jack couldn't wait to get home. Before breakfast one morning I went for a stroll along the seafront at Durban. It was absolutely lovely. The weather was magnificent, the trees, shrubs, the buildings, everything about the place was pristine clean and beautiful. I returned to our hotel to find Jack sitting in the front lounge writing a letter home. We exchanged greetings and I asked him if he was all right. He replied: 'Charlie, I'll tell you a secret ... I wish I was back home at Ashington.'

I remember one day we found ourselves beating Sunderland by four clear goals at Roker Park. About ten minutes into the second half, Jack was getting annoyed with Mitch and me for not showing any urgency in our play. He was yelling: 'Come on, lads! Come on - remember the 9-1.' That was the record score held in derby games by Sunderland. It just about describes the rivalry at that time. We eventually won by 6-1.

One morning in the early 1950s, Jack arrived at St James' for training in a motor car. You can imagine the speculation among the players: 'How can he afford that? Has he won the Pools, or what?' It transpired that the car was a gift from an ardent supporter and transport contractor from Westerhope. Later that same year, the firm presented Jack with a bus with which he began a bus-hire service, calling the bus 'The Ashington Flyer'. He also acquired a fireplace shop on Ashington's main street, and endorsed football boots.

For all his wonderful record at Newcastle, he was an extremely modest and shy man. When he went to the pictures in Ashington, he always waited until the lights were turned down low before he entered the cinema.

In the late Fifties, I worked part-time for James Diball, a builders' merchant. James was a Newcastle fanatic and his personal hero was Jackie Milburn. It didn't matter where James was, but if Jackie's name was mentioned he would leap to his feet and cry: 'Prince John. Prince John. That's my boy!' Jimmy's son Colin is a sports journalist with the *Daily Mirror* in the north east.

I was joined in the team bath by Jackie shortly after he had returned from playing in England's ill-fated squad in the 1950 World Cup in Rio. I asked him how he had enjoyed South America. 'Charlie,' he said, 'I watched a group of young boys using oranges as footballs on the beach. And they would only be aged between six and ten. But the control they showed, juggling and keeping the oranges in the air with their bare feet was uncanny. They were magic - born ball-players. And if they can turn out youngsters like that then teams from that area will be unbeatable.' Jack was right there, wasn't he.

Who said Jack Milburn couldn't head the ball?
Top photo shows him heading a goal at Roker Park for England against Wales, 1949.
And that's another beauty against Man United a year or two later at St James' Park.

Walker, Harvey and Mitchell were dedicated followers of fashion.

95

My Dad, Charles snr, presents me with an award at his club, Heaton RAOB,
as Bob Stokoe and Reg Davies look on in 1955

GORDON HUGHES, 1956

Gordon made his Newcastle debut against Manchester United, then nicknamed the Busby Babes, along with fullback Dick Keith. They both played well, but Gordon was outstanding against England internationals Duncan Edwards and Roger Byrne. On the following Wednesday we played Morton in Scotland, and Gordon broke his leg. When he eventually returned to the game after a lengthy absence, he was never the same player; he seemed to 'carry' his leg. I used to get annoyed when the crowd got at him - even though it was usually good natured. What a waste of a talent! I can still remember his debut: skill, pace, a big heart ... great stuff.

ALF McMICHAEL

Alf had joined us from Linfield in 1949 and spent nearly fourteen years with the Magpies. He never had it easy in the early days as he tried to break into the first team. In turn, he had to displace Doug Graham, then Bobby Corbett and, in 1955, arguably the best of the trio, Ron Batty. Alf always looked comfortable on the ball and never shirked a tackle. He formed an excellent partnership with Dick Keith, both for us and for the Northern Ireland national side. I roomed with Alf on several occasions and found him to be quiet and reserved. He won forty caps for Ireland, a club record for international duties, and played 431 games for Newcastle.

TICKET TOUTS

During our great FA Cup runs of the Fifties, tickets for the big game were always at a premium. At that time United were averaging 50,000 for a home match. but the FA allocation was only about 20,000 for the final - clearly not enough to satisfy the demands of our supporters.

It was in this climate that the players and officials of the club were being approached by the ticket touts offering ten to twenty times their face value.

Two men emerged as specialists: Tom Brown of Durham, and Chips Rose of Newcastle who was also a pools promoter in Ireland.

I first met Chips in a Jesmond pub called the *Cradle Well*. He asked me if I knew anyone with spare tickets to sell, to which I replied: 'I've enough problems getting tickets for the whole family. But, I'll tell you what ... I'll ask the other players and then put you in touch.'

Chips was always immaculately dressed, from his Homburg hat down to the spats on his shoes. Apart from his interest in cup tickets, he was a fervent fan of the Magpies and attended many away games, often travelling with the offical United party.

One bright and breezy afternoon, while waiting for Ernie Taylor outside a restaurant on Northumberland Street, I was joined by Chips. As we were chatting Ernie arrived and at that precise moment a lady was pasing by. Chips doffed his hat in a chivalrous greeting. But he had forgotten that he kept his spare cup-tickets inside the brim of his hat.

There was complete chaos as the wind took hold of the precious tickets, spreading then far and wide. Several passers by stopped to help Chips to retrieve them as they swirled around C&A then over the busy road to Marks & Spencer.

The restaurant was called the *Rendezvous*, but I never found out why he was called 'Chips'.

BOBBY ROBSON

I first met Bob in 1958 when he was in his early days at West Bromwich. This was the way it happened ...

I was waiting on the platform at York railway station for a connection to Newcastle. A personable young man introduced himself, saying he was a keen Magpie supporter. I shook hands with him and asked his name.

'Bobby Robson - I've just joined West Brom.'

We had a couple of beers in the buffet bar and travelled back to Newcastle together. Bobby was still living in county Durham.

That was the last time I talked to him until August, 1992. Newcastle were playing Sporting Lisbon in a pre-season game at st James' Park. As I entered the ground Bob was talking to a group of fans outside the players' entrance.

As I passed I shouted out: 'Hello, Bob.'

He turned and looked at me and shrugged his shoulders. Obviously he had not recognised me.

I then said: 'York Railway Station, 1958, Munich Air Disaster. I bought the drinks.'

He smiled and said: 'Hello, Charlie. How are you?' Then he turned to one of his companions and said: 'I used to follow these lads, you know.'

I think I detected a note of pride in his voice.

MUNICH AIR DISASTER, 1958

My last game for Newcastle United was against Manchester United. We lost by six goals to one. The Busby Babes as they were then known completely outclassed Newcastle. Their team was: Wood, Foulkes, Byrne, Colman, Jones, Edwards, Berry, Whelan, Taylor, Viollet and Pegg.

The following are extracts from the *Daily Telegraph*, written by Michael Parkinson, following the tragedy at Munich.

I reported the first game Manchester United played after the Munich air disaster - it was against Sheffield Wednesday. On the pitch, the Sheffield players might as well have played in ballet shoes so careful were they not to bruise their opponents or in any way offend the multitude. It wasn't a football match - it was a demonstration of grief.

But what Sheffield Wednesday learned on that occasion, and other teams were quick to understand, was that the odds and sods managed by Jimmy Murphy neither expected nor wanted to be handled like porcelain.

Jimmy Murphy's most significant contribution to the rebuilding of the team was to sign Ernie Taylor from Blackpool. There wasn't much of Ernie Taylor. Nowadays he'd probably fail the medical. But what he possessed was the combative spirit of a fighting bull; the cunning of a cat burglar; and the kind of skills with a football which made you gibber with delight. He was what used to be called 'a ball-juggling inside-forward'. Once upon a time *all* clubs had one. Nowadays they are as rare as wingers who can dribble.

His greatest ability was to unlock a defence with one pass. The distance didn't matter. Like Johnny Haynes, he had a range-finder in his toe caps.

Ernie was at the end of his career when he came to United from Blackpool, but he had enough left in him to orchestrate a glorious finale.

Some indication of the task facing Murphy and Taylor was that when the programme was printed for the first game after the crash, the United team consisted of eleven blank spaces.

Jimmy Murphy has never been given the accolade he deserved ... forgotten by revisioinst historians ... Ernie Taylor was his mouthpiece on the pitch.

GRANTED A FREE TRANSFER

In 1957, Stan Seymour said I could conduct my own move after being granted a free transfer. I was then employed full-time as a sales rep in the building trade, and had no desire to move house.

After talks with Charlie Mitten, then player-manager at Mansfield, I decided to join them. Mitten agreed my terms and said I could travel to matches on the Friday or Saturday morning.

I captained Mansfield for about a season, but sustained an injury which caused me to retire from football completely in 1958.

A few weeks after my decision to pack in, I received a phone call from Charlie Mitten. It transpired that he was ringing from my own house. 'What are you doing there, Charlie?' I asked.

'Oh, I'm just wasting a bit of time, waiting for the result of my application.'

'Application for what?'

'Oh, of course, you don't know - I've applied for the manager's job at Newcastle!'

After getting over my initial shock, I returned home from my office, enjoyed the rest of the evening, then I drove Mitten back to his hotel in the centre of the city. Several Newcastle directors were waiting in the hotel lounge to tell him that he was to be offered the job.

Charlie Mitten looked surprised and said he would see me the following evening. When we met again he said: ' How would *you* like to be head coach at St James'?'

'Yes please,' I said, 'but what about the salary?'

A figure was named which I refused. 'Well what figure have you in mind?' he asked.

I told him and he gasped. 'Bugger me, Charlie, you want more than *I'm* getting!'

'Well, that is what I think I am worth. If you don't then you have to get someone else.' After that meeting coaching was never mentioned.

'CHARLIE, I KEEP SEEING GHOSTS'

Although all of my former colleagues at Newcastle had left, I still had a soft spot for the club. I was really pleased when Joe Harvey got what he richly deserved when he was appointed manager in 1962 after Norman Smith had spent a short time as caretaker-manager.

I called in to see Joe in his office after he had settled in. 'Hello, there, Joe. And how are you coping with your new job?'

'Oh, Charlie, don't ask. I keep seeing ghosts on the pitch.'

'Ghosts!'

'When one of our players gets the ball, I expect him to do certain things with it like they did when you and me were playing, but it just doesn't happen. Why is that, Charlie?'

'That team is long gone, Joe. OK so there will never be one like it. But now you will have to come to terms with your present lads. They are Newcastle United now.'

STAN ANDERSON

Stan holds the unique record of having captained Newcastle, Sunderland and Middlesbrough. He was a classy wing-half who always had all the time in the world on the ball. He had the full range of talents and was an England player who should have gained a lot more caps.

I first played against Stan in 1951 when he was only eighteen years old, and we have been friends ever since. Off the field he was a quiet unassuming man, and after his playing career ended he went into the managerial side and was a great coach. When Stan was manager at Bolton he signed a Yugoslavian midfield player.. 'That fella can play a bit, Boss,' said one of his regular players. 'No he can't,' said Stan, 'but he can pass a ball accurately.'

Allchurch will help Newcastle United to move up in League

I HAD a very informative chat with Charlie Mitten, manager of my former club, Newcastle United, during the week and Charlie made no secret of the fact that he has a high regard for 17-year-old Matt Doherty, of Derry City.

Charlie is anxious to build up a powerful youth team and second string over the next couple of years in addition to his immediate programme which has made a good jump forward with the signature of the brilliant Welsh inside forward, Ivor Allchurch.

Charlie believes he will now have as strong a team as any other and if he can avoid further injuries Newcastle are expected to move right up the table.

Meanwhile mighty Arsenal are riding high and it is a tribute both to their strength and their goodwill that they have made no bones about five of their players being picked for international duty in the Wales v. Scotland match—a policy to be admired.

Mitten and George Swindin have a common policy for they took their jobs knowing that they had little to lose and were able to make a general clearing-up and a fresh start.

Strong defence

Peter Doherty also adopted the same idea when he went to Bristol City and yesterday signed John Crossan, the Coleraine inside forward.

Peter was most impressed with this Derry boy when sitting alongside me at the Gold Cup semi-final between Coleraine and Derry City.

Talking of Peter, the outstanding lesson from last week's fine international match was the strength of the defensive system he has perfected with the Irish team.

This was one of two main points for the Soccer student and Ireland are, without doubt, able to take on any team in the world at present—particularly under heavy conditions.

CHARLIE MITTEN

This is what Jack Milburn had to say about Mitten in his weekly column.

'Now tell me the truth, Jackie ... can
you see any ghosts out there?'

'HOW MANY RULES ARE THERE?'

Looking back, Joe Harvey had been groomed by Stan Seymour for taking charge at Newcastle, but first of all Joe had to acquire his FA Coaching Certificate. I had obtained mine in 1951, but it was two years later when Joe and I travelled to Lilleshall in Shropshire to attend his first coaching session organised by Walter Winterbottom.

On the way down by train, Joe plied me with all sorts of questions. 'Have you studied the referees' handbook, Joe?' I asked him 'And the charter?'

'No. Why?'

'Because you will need to pass the referees' examinations, as well as the practical and theory papers before you are awarded your badge. For example, one of the questions you may be asked is how many rules are there in football?'

Joe just scratched his head. 'Charlie, man, there must be hundreds.'

But it did not matter one iota to me whether Joe knew or not, I knew personally that Joe was the best in the business as a captain and as a man-manager that I ever encountered. Joe's initial apprenticeship as a manager took him to Workington and Barrow in the then third division before taking over at Newcastle where he spent thirteen years as manager.

They say behind every good man there is a good woman, and Joe's wife Ida was a charming lady with a strong personality of her own. She supported Joe one hundred per cent with anything connected with Newcastle United.

Ida was to be seen at all the first team games. Supporters loved this straight-talking Yorkshire woman. A sports journalist once made the remark: 'I was talking to Newcastle's boss the other day.' 'Oh, aye,' came the reply, 'did she have Joe with her?'

'WITHOUT BEING KICKED'

Len Shackleton became a sports journalist after he retired from playing. He was in attendance at St James' to watch a game between Newcastle and Derby County, in the mid-Sixties. Derby were then managed by Tim Ward, a former England half-back and a renowned fierce tackler.

Joe Harvey invited me to join both managers for a chat and a drink before the game. We were in the foyer when the press door opened and in walked Len Shackleton.

Len looked across and began to walk towards us. When he was about two metres away he suddenly stopped dead in his tracks, saying, 'Do you know, fellas, this is the closest I have ever been to you three without being kicked up in the air.'

Len was reporting on a Newcastle home game when Liam Tuohy, United's Irish winger, from only three yards missed an open goal. The goalie was stranded, but still Liam contrived to put the ball over the bar.

In his match report Len wrote: 'Liam Tuohy, United's winger, will probably be still wondering how he came to miss that open goal; he would possibly want to kick himself - but then again, he might miss!'

My eldest daughter Lesley was travelling back from holiday on the plane with her husband. Sitting opposite them were two men. One had his suitcase down beside the seat and the name clearly marked read ... *LF SHACKLETON.*

Lesley asked him if he was the footballer of that name and he nodded. She then told him that she was my daughter. 'Charlie Crowe is *your* father,' said Len, barely able to contain his laughter, He rolled up his trouser leg to reveal an imaginary scar. 'That's where he kicked me!'

GEORGE EASTHAM

When Newcastle United were winning their three FA cup finals the players were still on a basic wage of £12 a week. It was indirectly because of the Magpies that the ceiling was lifted, making for the *sky*'s-the-limit type of wages which footballers earn today. And it was all because of a slim blond-haired lad called George Eastham.

I played behind George on his debut for United at home to Luton in 1956. He was only nineteen years of age, but already showed a lot of promise. A feature of his play was his pin-point pass and all-round work rate. Len White said George's passes could be likened to the threading of a needle.

In 1960 he was at odds with manager Charlie Mitten, and asked for a transfer which was refused. He took Newcastle United to the High Court, winning his case, and changing the face of soccer forever.

Off the field he was quiet and thoughtful, playing 139 games for United and scoring 34 goals; he was also capped for England nineteen times.

ALBERT SCANLON

Charlie Mitten signed his nephew Albert Scanlon from Manchester United in 1960. Mitten phoned me and asked if I would meet Albert and introduce him to the area.

My first impression was that Albert was still trying to readjust from the Munich air crash which had killed so many of his mates. So in his early games for us he was a long way from his recognised form.

During one home game two fans had a go at him. 'That Scallion gets worse.' 'It's not Scallion, man, it's Scanlon.' 'Scanlon or Scallion - they both bring tears to my eyes.'

'SEE HOW FAST HE CAN LIMP'

Joe Harvey was the longest serving manager in Newcastle's history. As a captain he always played the game hard and, as a manager, expected his players to do the same. If he was asked what qualities he liked most in a centre-half he would always prefer the stopper to the ball-player.

United were having a pre-match talk prior to an important European cup-tie. Joe took John McGrath to one side and said: 'John, I would like to see early in the game, how fast their centre-forward can *limp!*'

Joe Harvey was often the butt of many of United's practical jokes. He was receiving treatment from physio Alec Mutch on a pulled muscle one morning in the medical room when Ernie Taylor got his eye on him.

Joe was lying face down on the treatment table, naked, except for a towel draped over his shoulders. On the shelf was a bottle of ether. On odd occasions we had seen the effects when ether came into contact with a player's private parts.

Ernie asked me to to disrtact Alec's attention which I did, lurng him out of the room. Ernie sneaked in unnoticed by Joe and squeezed from a piece of cotton wool a small amount of ether above Joe's backside. Then Ernie got out, fast. Next door we had perpared a slipper bath full of cold water. But cold water does not ease the pain - it makes it a hundred times worse!

When the ether began to take effect, Joe let out a shriek which could be heard at the Gallowgate End. He came rushing into the dressing room, shouting and screaming with pain and rage.

He was directed to the bath of cold water. But after his initial plunge into the bath he let out another roar of agony. I will not repeat what he said next.

'HUSH, CHARLIE, IT'S A SECRET'

In the early 1960s I had occasion to go to Glasgow as the firm I worked for had booked a trade stand at Kelvin Hall for three weeks. I was to organise it. It was while travelling home for the weekend on the train that I spotted a newspaper headline which forecast that Newcastle were looking to sign Willie Stevenson of Glasgow Rangers.

On the last Monday while waiting for the train at Newcastle Central, I bumped into Joe Harvey and two directors: Stan Seymour and Fenton Braithwaite.

'Where are you off to, Charlie?' asked Joe.

'Oh, I've got a spot of business to do up in Glasgow.'

'Fine,' said Stan. 'Why don't you join us in the dining car for lunch.'

It was over dessert that I asked the question: 'And what are you going up to Glasgow for? I suppose it's to sign Willie Stevenson from Rangers.'

Seymour looked horrified. 'Hush, Charlie,' he said, looking around him to make sure no one had heard. 'That is a secret.'

'You must be joking, Stan,' I said. 'Everybody in Scotland knows. It's in all their papers.'

The United trio were very upset at this news. Stan turned to Joe and said: 'Obviously a leak somewhere along the line, Joe. We shall have to find out when we get back.'

On the Wednesday, the United party watched Stevenson play for Rangers in a reserve match at Aidrie. But they decided *not* to make an offer for the player.

He was transferred to Liverpool on the Thursday and made his debut against Newcastle United the following Saturday.

'NO AMATEUR PLAYER IS WORTH IT'

After I left Mansfield, I was approached to take over as manager of Whitley Bay FC in 1959. At the end of our first season we finished bottom of the Northern League. I obviously felt that the players we had were clearly not good enough.

Before the start of the new season I had a word with our chairman, Jack Hedworth and his fellow director, Arthur Clark, whose knowledge and contacts in amateur football were invaluable.

I told them that I was interested in signing Laurie Brown, the Bishop Auckland centre-half. Then the question arose: could the club afford his expenses? which then averaged at about two or three pounds a week for our own players.

After Arthur had left, the chairman gave me permission to offer Laurie the maximum of ten pounds a week. I passed on this information to Laurie who said he was interested and would think it over. But he rang a few weeks later saying that he had agreed better terms with Bishop Auckland. I wished him all the best, but I was bitterly disappointed.

Midway through my second season the directors had been discussing finances and asked me to join them. I was asked to economise on one player's expenses. 'That is out out of the question,' I retorted. 'What would have happened if we had signed Laurie Brown and then gone back on our word and cut *his* expenses?'

'Who gave you permission to offer money like that to amateurs?' asked a director. 'Surely no amateur footballer is worth that kind of money.'

When he calmed down I told him that our chairman had authorised the offer.

Laurie eventually signed professional terms with Northampton and was later transferred to Arsenal then Spurs in deals worth £100,000.

Bob Hardisty shakes hands with John Mitten, son of Newcastle United manager, Charlie Mitten. John is Whitley Bay's outside-left. With them is the Bay centre-forward, Ray Oliver, and the club manager, Charlie Crowe.

According to a local rag, I 'turned down a handsome offer as a player by Blyth Spartans so that I could go to the coast team'. The Whitley Bay squad Back left: H Ross trainer, Brian Oakley, Stafford Newham Edgar, Walton, Robson, Browell.
Front: Stoker, Johnson, Duffy, Bell and Mitten. On the left, Ray Oliver was a great old pro; we have remained in close contact ever since.

LEN WHITE, 1953 - 1962

Len was always a personal friend of mine straight from the time he signed for the Magpies. Curiously, Len was instrumental in Newcastle's exit from the FA Cup in 1953.

He was then one of eight pitmen who played for second division Rotherham who beat us 3-1 in one of the early rounds.

Off the field, Len was like the three Newcastle No 9s who had preceded him: Wayman, Stubbins and Milburn, all quiet, unassuming men who never sought the limelight.

On the park it was all very different. Len was volatile, strong, and excellent in the air for a small man. He just bubbled and buzzed all over the front line, popping up where least expected. His main asset was change of pace. Few footballers have the art of appearing to be at full speed then stepping up a gear and cruising away from opponents.

Len really came to the fore when he was switched to centre-forward on a permanent basis, playing alongside Ivor Allchurch and George Eastham, making a formidable trio that may never be bettered.

In my opinion, Len White was the best in the business from 1957-62, and still, amazingly, did not get an England cap.

Len played 268 games for Newcastle, scoring 153 goals. A strike rate of 57 per cent.

'CROWE SENT OFF'

I played in a charity match at South Shields in 1966. It was an entertaing game with Mitchell showing his dribbling skills, and Jackie Milburn proving that at forty-two he had lost none of his speed or shooting power. Stan Anderson was another to shine that night. But late in the second half I began to tire. I asked the ref: 'How long to go?' 'Two minutes,' he replied.

'Well, you have sent me off, OK.' I said, walking wearily from the pitch. As I left the field a local reporter asked what was wrong.

'The referee has sent me off,' I replied jokingly.

In the local newspaper the next day the sports column read: *'Crowe sent off in Friendly'*. The reporter obviously did not have a sense of humour.

'CROWE FOR EGYPT'

In 1967 I was employed by Crossleys builders merchants. My wife Ruth rang me at work to say that Walter Winterbottom had offered me a coaching position with Zamalek FC in Cairo. She was so pleased that she actually sang to me over the line: *"See the Pyramids along the Nile"* (a 1950s pop song).

My agent then was Ken Wolstenholme of Inter Club Sports who arranged meetings for me with the Zamalek officials. Arrangements were made for Ruth and myself and twin boys; we would fly to Cairo and sign a three-year contract in Arabic and English.

Walter had recomended me for several jobs in the past, but this was something special. I gave three month's notice to my employers. When I was saying farewell to my friends I told Frank Brennan I would send for him to join me when I got settled. A local paper headline read: 'Crowe for Egypt'.

I walked into a Tynside pub a few days before take off and one wag shouted at me, waving his newspaper: 'Hey, look at this, lads, *'Crowe for Egypt'*. Canny swap, eh.'

But the day before we were due to fly, Israeli planes bombed all of Egypt's airfields and started the Five-day War.

It had been a lovely dream while it lasted.

Interclub Sports Services Ltd.

DIRECTORS: GEORGE STURRUP
KENNETH WOLSTENHOLME
STAN WHITEHORN
SECRETARY: E. STURRUP

ASSOCIATED WITH
CONTINENTAL DEPORTES.
(CASILDO OSES)
OFFICES IN:
BUENOS AIRES
SAN MARTIN 491·5°·17.
TELEPHONE: 318760
329265
325584
MEXICO DF.
HAMBURGO 25 A y B
TELEPHONE: 464281
465698
465642
MADRID
SERRANO 230 N.
TELEPHONE: 2598958

135 NOTTING HILL GATE,
LONDON. W. 11.

TELEPHONE: BAYSWATER 8767/9467

CABLES & TELEGRAMS. ▮▮▮▮▮▮▮▮▮▮

Refgoal, London, W.11.

Mr. Charles Crowe,
"Somerville,"
Netherton Training School,
Stannington,
near Morpeth. Northumberland.

June 20, 1967.

Dear Charlie,

Many thanks for your letter. The last word I had from Egypt was a couple of days before the shooting started. I wrote a letter in return, but whether that ever reached its destination is a matter for conjecture.

I think it is best to let the dust of war settle before writing to them again, and in the meantime, I have sent your qualifications to Australia.

With every good wish -- and thank goodness you hadn't gone out to Cairo!

Yours sincerely,

(signature)

(Kenneth Wolstenholme)

— 'They thought it was all over!
It is now.'

107

JACK MILBURN'S TESTIMONIAL, 1967

Jack got his overdue benefit match in May, 1967. Before the big event, two teams of ageing players took took to the field.

The oppostion kicked off and Len Shackleton came towards me with the ball. I tried to make it easy for him. 'Through my legs, Len. Come on.' But he took no notice and hit a daisy-cutter fully thirty yards to Tom Finney on the left-wing. Finney took the pace from Shack's pass and dropped the ball stone dead, sold Bob Cowell a perfect dummy, raced to the byeline and crossed to the far post where it was taken out by Jack Fairbrother.

I turned to Shack, asking: 'Why didn't you put that ball through my legs?'

'After all these years, Charlie, I still don't trust you.'

In the second half, Len bent a shot from an impossible angle into the net past a startled Fairbrother. He then turned to the press-box, pointing to the number on his shirt, as though to say: 'Get it right, lads. The name is *Shackleton*.'

But what I remember most of that period was in the run-up to the game. A full one month before the event I trained at St James' two nights a week to try to get into some kind of shape. After all, I was pushing forty-three and not in mint condition.

One night I had two hours along with Jack Milburn in the gym. 'That's it, Jack,' I said after a long gruelling session, 'I'm away for a shower.'

'Hold on, Charlie,' said Jack clutching a ball. 'Let me have five minutes shooting practice. You can keep goal.'

So we went outside where a goal area was marked in white paint outside the gymnasium wall. It was about eight o'clock at night and the light was not good.

The first thing that I knew after taking up position was a terrible thud about a foot from my head. Then the ball hurtled back to Jack. I had never seen the ball, and got out of the firing line immediately.

'Hey, Jack, do you not know you could have killed me.' I still say to this day that if the ball had struck me in the face and my head had hit the wall, it would have killed me stone dead.

As I walked away, Jack was still hitting balls at the wall with terrific speed with either foot. He was the most natural striker of the ball I have ever seen.

Around the same time, Scottish and Newcastle Breweries had opened a new public house just outside the ground called the *Magpie*. The bar fitters and interior decorators were run by a man called Tom Henderson.

Tom rang me saying he wanted to make a feature point in the pub, and did I know if any of the players would lend their international caps to display in a cabinet for a while.

Frank Brennan (Scotland), Alf McMichael (Ireland), and Reg Davies (Wales), readily agreed. But I had trouble trying to contact Jack Milburn to borrow his England gear.

I eventually got through to him; he invited me to his house in Ashington for a chat and a cup of coffee. After introducing him to Jack, Tom gave him all the details of his plans for the project.

While Tom had been talking, Jack had been nodding his head and he immediately agreed.

Jack got to his feet and shouted from the lounge to his wife, Laura: 'Hey, Laura, where are me England caps just noo? Are they underneath the bed or are they still in the garage?'

The thirteen irreplaceable England caps were in the garage.

Puskas turns on the power

Newcastle-Sunderland 1, International XI 3

THE crowd who stayed to the end in heavy rain will always be grateful to Ferenc Puskas and Bobby Charlton. This was no jaunt for them. They went out of their way to put on a serious show. They succeeded magnificently.

Perhaps it was the all-white Real Madrid like strip which made Puskas play as though in the European Cup. Perhaps, after the tremendous welcome he received, he knew he had to do his stuff.

His first appearance in the North-East will be talked about for years.

With a suggestion of co-operation from the opposition, Milburn scored the first goal of the game.

Later he retired amid a tremendous roar of farewell. From then on it was the internationals who entertained.

George Eastham equalised from an Alan Suddick pass. Then Charlton — it's clear there is Milburn blood in this lad — unleashed a power drive reminiscent of Jackie to put his side ahead.

The crowd were happier still in the second half for they can now claim they have seen Puskas score. He got his goal from a chance created by George Mulhall and Pat Crerand.

Newcastle-Sunderland.—Marshall; Irwin, Clark; Eliott, Kinnell, Iley; Herd, Davies, Milburn (capt.), Martin, Robson B. Sub.: Craig.

Internationals. — Waiters; Armfield, Brennan; Crerand, McGrath, Stiles; Suddick, Eastham, Charlton (capt.), Puskas, Mulhall.

DOUG WEATHERALL

It's like old times as Jackie meets those Wembley wonders again

Milburn

Thanks, Jackie ... and the Tyneside fans will say it 50,000 times

By KEN McKENZIE

TYNESIDE FANS will say a golden thank you to Jackie Milburn, when their former idol has his testimonial match at St. James's Park tonight.

All stand tickets went days ago and the paddock is almost a sell-out as well.

Milburn is already assured of £2,700 from ticket sales, and with the crowd likely to reach 50,000, this figure should be boosted well towards the £10,000 mark.

The evening will provide a sporting mixed grill to whet the appetite of every fan.

As well as the soccer attractions, there will be British Lightweight boxing champion Maurice Cullen doing a work out with George Bowes, and a track mile with world-class Jimmy Alder, Ernie Pomfret and other area stars taking part.

Appreciation

We had evidence of Tyneside appreciation to a favourite when Bob Mitchell's testimonial match drew a gate of 40,960 in October, 1961. He received a cheque for £6,198, which I believe swelled to £7,000 on ticket receipts and donations.

The gates open at 5.30 p.m., and the 15th/19th Royal Hussars Band, world famous and just back from West Germany, will be entertaining from about 6.15 p.m.

The first Soccer match, in which the great United Cup-winning team of 1951, with later medallist Alf McMichael in for lone absentee George Robledo, will play other former favourites, including six-goals "Shack," cheeky-chappie Ivor Broadis, and my greatest winger Tom Finney, starts at 7 p.m.

MILBURN in his playing day

It was an emotional occasion

'YOU DID KICK ME

I was a guest speaker for Blyth Rotarians in 1980. After being introduced to the chairman before my talk he told me, 'There is a gentleman in the audience tonight, an ex-professional footballer, who once played against you,'

I failed to remember the chap's name, but when I stood up I said: 'I believe there is someone in the hall who played against me - would that gentleman mind standing up after he has put his crutches to one side.'

This fellow actually leapt to his feet, shouting: 'Yes, it is true. You *did* kick me. In fact you broke my ankle.' He then related to the audience how it happened, describing in full detail about the free-kick which was given and how I had tackled him.

When I talked to him towards the end of the evening, he relived the incident again. But after a couple of drinks, all was forgiven.

'SEE STOKOE AS A THREAT'

In 1988, I was at a sports function with a group of former Newcastle United players who were talking shop. Sunderland and Bob Stokoe had just parted company, and he was a free agent.

I said: 'Why don't Newcastle United employ Bob in some capacity; he still has a lot to offer with his coaching and managerial experience, plus his contacts in the football world.'

At that time Willie McFaul was United's manager. I suggested that Bob, if he was interested, could be of some value to Willie. I knew Bob was slightly emabarrassed by me bringing up the subject while he was present.

Dave Hilley replied: 'That would never happen. Willie would see Bob as a threat to his job.'

Why do some managers *not* want to surround themselves with first class people?

PROLOGUE

And that just about wraps things up. I have had a rich varied life and come out of it smelling of roses, as the saying goes.

Oh, I haven't got a Bentley or Porsche in the garage. In fact I haven't even got a garage. But I manage to get around on my pensioners' Metro ticket. And Longbenton to St James' Park is just a ten-minute train ride away.

Not that I get there to see the matches anymore. There was a time when my old friend Peter Mallinger was on the Newcastle board when he made sure I had an ample supply of tickets for myself and a couple of friends to sit in the directors' box. And at half-time me and big Frank Brennan would go back to the warmth of the hospitality room where Frank would prove to all and sundry that he had not lost his propensity for eating gigantic cream cakes,

The pity was that, at that time, Newcastle United were in the doldrums of the old second division; their loyal supporters robbed of the chance to see the great players of Arsenal and Man United. Fans were starved of the lifeblood of top-class football which is theirs by right.

But everything comes to those who wait, and Kevan Keagan proved the catalyst that was to shoot Newcastle to unimagined dizzy heights.

Sadly, those momentous years also saw a change of priorities and Peter Mallinger moved on. So now, with thousands of others, my view of St James' Park and the famous black & whites is determined by the size of a TV screen.

But I still have my contacts, and friends still stop me on the street to emphasise how much better the team of the early 1950s was compared to today. Like Joe Harvey, God bless him, the fans still see the ghost of Jackie Milburn, shirt flapping in the wind; Bob Mitchell going on another mazy dribble; and Ernie Taylor ... Ah!

The Jackie Milburn Memorial Trust came into being in 1991 "To help those in need with particular emphasis on the young disabled."

Each year since then we have made individual (and collective) awards up to £300, and in some cases donated a free week's holiday for the recipient and his/her family and carers.

To give some idea of those we have helped ... first was Paul Stearman, a Downs Syndrome laddie from Cramlington who had won medals at the Special Olympics; an award was made to Newcastle-based 'Our Lady of Lourdes' Deaf School Drama Group who were also given a tour of St James' and seats for a home game; the appropriately named Nicky Milburn of Throckley - a seven-year-old boy with a rare bone disease - was another to benefit ... and so on.

So when Charlie Crowe came up with the idea of putting his wealth of knowledge about the game of football down on paper together with many anecdotes concerning legends like Jackie Milburn, Len Shackleton and Stanley Matthews, the trustees thought that was an ideal way to boost our kitty. Especially as we don't go in for what you might call major fund-raising events.

The fund was set up from the royalties of my book *Jackie Milburn in Black and White* and was launched from St James' Park. Some of the founder members are pictured in front of the Milburn Stand: George Luke, Bob Cowell, myself, Frank Brennan and Charlie. Sadly, Bob and Frank are no longer with us.

But the Trust goes on and will benefit each time a fan buys *A Crowe amongst the Magpies*. If you would like to donate money, write to me, Mike Kirkup, 5 Aqua Terrace, Newbiggin by the Sea, Northumberland, NE64 6PB, or ring 01670 855749. (*Charity No. 100340*)